TRANSNATIONAL BUSINESS AND CORPORATE CULTURE

PROBLEMS AND OPPORTUNITIES

edited by
STUART BRUCHEY
ALLAN NEVINS PROFESSOR EMERITUS
COLUMBIA UNIVERSITY

T0346785

THE SOCIAL CONSEQUENCES OF ECONOMIC RESTRUCTURING IN THE TEXTILE INDUSTRY

CHANGE IN A SOUTHERN MILL VILLAGE

CYNTHIA D. ANDERSON

Routledge
Taylor & Francis Group

LONDON AND NEW YORK

First published 2000 by Garland Publishing, Inc.

2 Park Square, Milton Park, Abingdon, Oxon OX14 4RN
711 Third Avenue, New York, NY 10017, USA

Routledge is an imprint of the Taylor & Francis Group, an informa business

First issued in paperback 2016

Library of Congress Cataloguing-in-Publication Data

Anderson, Cynthia D.
   The social consequences of economic restructuring int he textile indus-
try : change in a southern mill village / Cynthia D. Anderson.
       p. cm. — (Transnational business and corporate culture)
   Includes bibliographical references and index.
   ISBN 0-8153-3622-5 (alk. paper)
       1. Textile workers—North Carolina—Kannapolis. 2. Textile indus-
try—North Carolina—Kannapolis. 3. International trade—Social
aspects—North Carolina—Kannapolis. 4. Fieldcrest Cannon Inc. I.
Title. II. Series.

HD8039.T42 U635 2000
305.9'677'0975671—dc21

                                                          00-057808

ISBN 978-0-8153-3622-8 (hbk)
ISBN 978-1-138-99620-5 (pbk)

Nathalee Lackey Royster
1912-1997

To a strong and loving woman who demonstrated
the value of education and independence.

Contents

Acknowledgments

Deep gratitude goes to members of the Kannapolis community—the textile workers, ex-workers, activists, and community leaders. I also extend appreciation to the professors and librarians at North Carolina State University School of Textiles. I owe special gratitude to a key mentor, Michael Schulman, who continues to support my professional advancement.

A strong network of friends and family supported the completion of this book. Love to Jackie Litt, Jim McGlew, Amy Foster, Donna Lancaster, Kristen Myers, and Vinnie Roscigno. Thanks to my family, for growing with me. I cannot express the dedication of my family—the Andersons, Ervins, Kochs, Roysters, and Woods. Over the years, our bonds have strengthened in different and special ways. I am extremely grateful for each and every one of you.

Preface

I grew up in the foothills of the North Carolina mountains, surrounded by traditional southern industry—farming, furniture, and textiles. The work my parents did fit this context. My father was a furniture designer, and my mother provided economic assistance through a series of temporary jobs in teaching and human service. Together, with the support of a tight-knit extended family, they defied the sociological odds and raised three children fortunate enough to succeed their class position.

Pop recently took "early retirement"; the traditional skills of a furniture designer are not necessary in the modern, computerized, mass production industry. Mom continues to work in social services, of late shifting from counseling bereaved Hospice families to assisting local unemployed workers in collecting compensation. Despite skills, experience, and advanced education, her pay remains devastatingly low. Today, after years of critical training and reflection, I recognize that my parents' work experiences shaped my current research interests, feminist consciousness, and desire to teach.

My parents' hometown, much like the community of Kannapolis, suffers from severe deindustrialization. Furniture factories and textile plants continue to decrease their need for human labor. Few options exist for the many workers who have given their most productive years to local companies. In a nation with overall stable and relatively low unemployment, communities like these stand out and call for attention.

The structure of power and domination in southern communities is changing. Paternalistic control, typically portrayed as a form of traditional authority and benevolent protection of workers, is no longer dominant. With decreased need for skilled labor, company owners are not obligated to communities. No longer do they send workers home for holidays with hams and oranges. Formerly protected and isolated companies actively pursue global production and trade. Likewise, communities are now players on an international scale, with workers competing for jobs on a global level. New forms of class exploitation, racism, and sexism provide a contested terrain for community members.

My goal is to elucidate the linkages between large-scale social change in local-level outcomes; to expose the processes that create advantage and disadvantage for certain groups of people; to make real the often hidden lives of American workers, such as those in the textile mills, their struggles, defeats, and victories. This book does not offer advice for unemployed textile workers; nor does it make suggestions for community revitalization. However, readers will gain a better understanding of how global development, economic restructuring, and spatial relocation influence the everyday lives of American workers and families. Their stories, like those of many of us, are stories of endurance and passion.

THE SOCIAL CONSEQUENCES OF ECONOMIC RESTRUCTURING IN THE TEXTILE INDUSTRY

CHANGE IN A SOUTHERN MILL VILLAGE

Chapter One

An Introduction to Southern United States Textiles

The lives of early twentieth century southern United States textile workers may be characterized as a series of struggles. Production work was strenuous, requiring long hours in hot, noisy mills. Workers received low wages. Paternalist company owners controlled mill villages, leaving workers little independence in contrast to the farm lives they had forsaken. Yet we can find a glimmer of hope in histories of textile communities (Hall et al. 1987). For many southern textile workers, living and working in a mill village was upward mobility from farms, granting access to new amenities. Additionally, there was a comradeship among workers that did not exist to the same degree in farming communities—a comradeship that at times provided the solidarity needed for labor resistance. As evidenced by the General Strike of 1934, mill workers were not always passive victims of oppressive rule. Rather, they exhibited significant amounts of cultural autonomy and human agency (Hall et al. 1987).

Today, a visitor to a contemporary textile community in the South can observe physical evidence of the old system of paternalism. White-painted mill houses still surround the mills. The original owner's name remains evident around town, ensconced in the names of recreation centers, high schools, and libraries. However, a modern-day visitor who looks beyond these vestiges of paternalism will observe vast differences from the textile-mill community of the past. Mill villages are now incorporated towns. The mill, if it still exists, uses inventive technologies and labor processes. Regional industrialism has brought new industries, firms, and jobs to the area. New ethnic groups move in and out of the area. The community is no longer isolated; rather, it is integrated into a labor market that is regional and linked with systems that are global.

Contemporary conditions in southern textile-mill communities reflect the impacts of globalization, restructuring, and spatialization. Computerized equipment and just-in-time manufacturing are modernizing the production of fabric. Many family-owned companies are forming conglomerates by merging with other firms, both national and international. Imported textile goods, downward pressures on labor costs, plant shutdowns, modernization, and mergers are all part of current industry restructuring. Changes in technology and management have and continue to result in a significant reduction in the number of textile jobs. Where markets were once limited to the local geography, nation-state regulation (e.g., North American Free Trade Agreement and the General Agreement on Tariffs and Trade) promise to expand those markets to the global economy.

From a sociological perspective, these dynamic processes bring about a modification in the structure of power and domination in southern textile communities. Paternalistic control, typically portrayed as a form of traditional authority that provided benevolent protection to workers, is no longer dominant. With the decreased need for labor, textile company owners are not obligated to provide mill villages with housing, electricity, and water. Communities that once were protected and isolated are now players on an international scale, with workers competing for jobs on a global level.

The continuation of past patterns of oppression and the emergence of new forms constitute a puzzle in which one piece does not always fit cleanly to the others. What the puzzle is about is how old and new patterns of social inequality fit together. For sociologists concerned with social inequality, important research questions revolve around subordination, struggle, and the social consequences of change. As mills modernize, shut down, or move production overseas, workers and their households may experience unemployment, mortgage foreclosures, and out-migration. What are the social consequences of change for those southern textile workers? How have their jobs and lives changed because of changes in their workplaces and in their communities? What are the processes that perpetuate and alter inequality within southern textile-mill communities? To answer these and related questions, my research involves a multi-level analysis of the southern textile industry and, using a case study, focuses on a specific firm, its surrounding labor market area, and the workers within the community.

In this chapter, I ground the analyses of the social consequences of change in the southern textile industry in theories of paternalism and structural-exploitation. I use the concepts of globalization, restructuring, and spatialization to note weaknesses in these theories. In addition, I argue that the inadequacies with current theories are indicative of problems within the field of sociology as a whole. The discipline of sociology is increasingly fragmented into sections and sub-groups. Consequently, the interconnections between local and global processes are sometimes lost or forgotten. The social consequences of change are complex; to account for those complexities, both theory and method need to be multi-dimensional and focused on processes rather than outcomes.

ANALYZING SOUTHERN TEXTILE WORKERS: DOMINANT THEORETICAL ARGUMENTS

Two broad theoretical frameworks predominate sociological analyses of the social organization of southern textile communities and southern textile workers—paternalism and structural-exploitation. I present each frame by identifying its key concepts, assumptions, and relevant empirical studies found in the literature.

Paternalism

Paternalism refers to a system wherein one group dominates another under the guise of kindness, duty, and benevolent obligation (Jackman 1994). In the broadest sense, paternalism legitimizes traditional authority relationships between owners and workers in stereotypical company towns (Newby 1977). Labor historians and sociologists have applied the frame to analyze management-labor relations in a wide range of industrial communities (e.g., Burawoy 1979; Genovesse 1974; Newby 1977). In studies of the southern textile industry, paternalism refers not only to company control of land, buildings, goods, and services in the mill villages, but also to the ideology that overlays the relations between workers and mill owners (Frankel 1984; Freeze 1991; Janiewski 1985; McLaurin 1971; Newman 1978; Pope 1942). The paternalism framework is unique in its focus on authority relations, workers' lives, and culture as a means of arriving at conclusions of mill and community life.

There is a long tradition of scholarship about southern textile workers, mills, and mill communities that is based upon the paternalist frame of reference. In general, early scholarship focused on class relationships and emphasized worker dependence upon owners, elite control, worker subordination, and unionization struggles (e.g., Mitchell 1921; Thompson 1906). Most researchers assumed paternalism to be a benevolent institution that arose from a tradition of noblesse oblige by industrial elites, a tradition that was uncritically accepted by the masses of white, lower-class textile workers. Later researchers, including historians (Freeze 1991, 1994; Salmond 1995) and sociologists (McLaurin 1971; Pope 1942), focused on dynamic relationships in specific mill villages (e.g., Gastonia, NC), detailing life during particular moments of labor dissent and strikes (e.g., Carlton 1982; McLaurin 1971). These scholars argue that paternalism is more accurately characterized as the concentration of power in the hands of a small elite (Billings 1979; Carlton 1982; McLaurin 1971).

In general, paternalism is a concept that focuses on power relations and the links between the workplace and community, as well as connections between firms and their local labor markets. Within the paternalist

framework, analyses of social change in southern textile communities high-
light changes in traditional authority relations, in the culture of deference,
and in the spatial isolation of mill villages. Accordingly, major social consequences of change are seen as revolving around workplace and community integration. We find the best examples of this perspective in classic
studies of southern textiles, including Mitchell (1921), Thompson (1906),
and Potwin (1927). As these case studies demonstrate, the success of textile firms in the South emanated from a structure in which the elite owners
were obligated to provide for their workers, and the workers were required
to uncritically accept it. Beneficence and deference permeated both the
workplace and community, uniting members of these spheres into a cohe-
sive "family."

Not all scholars, however, view paternalism as a beneficial institution;
some criticize it as a weak explanation of social inequality in southern textile communities. As Simon (1991:81) states,

> Scholars have stretched the term so thin that it now has little clear
> meaning. Southern cotton mill paternalism has been defined as
> everything from kind fatherly stewardship (Mitchell 1921), to the
> complete control of rural industrial hamlets (McLaurin 1971), to
> the direct descendant of the Old South's master-slave relationship
> (Billings 1979; Cash 1941).

Additionally, as Jackman (1994) argues, paternalism has a significance that
extends into contemporary examples of control of the social relationships
between groups. Contemporary scholars seek to correct the concept's
shortcomings by representing paternalism as a complex relationship that
changes over time (Simon 1991) and as a complex mixture of processes,
including gender and race dynamics (Jackman 1994).

However, the major problem with the paternalism framework is that it
is relatively easy for researchers to revert to a form of sociological essentialism—describing workers as quiescent because their essential nature has
been warped by the cultural legacy of control in the company town. In this
view, the cultural legacy of deference continues to mold future generations
of workers (Newby 1977). While this analysis may be empirically correct
in some cases, in others it is an over-simplified conclusion that neglects the
broader social forces impacting textile firms, communities, and workers.

The value of the paternalism framework is that it focuses on people and
community-workplace interaction. Its fundamental weakness is its tendency towards one-dimensional cultural essentialism. To address this deficien-
cy, researchers of southern textile communities and workplaces need tools
that describe historical processes in terms that account for situationally
specific social relations. To this end, it is useful to adopt the concept of
embeddedness: that is, to locate individuals, groups, and structures in
social and spatial contexts (Anderson 1996). Applied to the paternalist

theoretical framework, embeddedness suggests that we root our analysis of communities and workplaces in industrial, national, and global contexts. For example, how have changes in the global economy affected textile firms and mill communities? Adopting the concept of embeddedness expands our understanding of social consequences to include the impacts of the economy, industry, and firm on workplace and community interactions.

Structural-exploitation

Structural-exploitation is the other dominant theoretical framework for sociological studies of southern textile workers and communities, and it stands in contrast to paternalism in that it focuses on the process of capital accumulation. A variety of specific approaches fall into this framework, united by the assumption that inequality is fundamentally the result of class conflicts over the distribution of surplus within the capitalist mode of production. Researchers using this framework argue that we need to examine the contexts that constrain the actions of individuals and focus on arenas such as industry, firm, labor market, and commodity system. In this view, workers are seen as relatively less powerful than owners and are thus subject to constraints from mechanisms which shape and control individual outcomes. For example, low wages, poor working conditions, little job mobility, stretch outs, blacklisting and so on are evidence of capitalist domination and control over workers. The structural-exploitation framework suggests that workers will resist oppression—in fact, they do revolt—but at least in the southern United States, capitalists and the state typically overpowered the workers (Hall et al. 1987; Stone and Heffner 1995).

Researchers of the southern textile industry who rely on this perspective have examined the determinants of peripheral capital accumulation (Wood 1986; 1991), the organization of regional economies and labor market composition (Penn and Leiter 1991), and the consequences of deindustrialization (Gaventa and Smith 1991). In contrast to the emphasis placed on traditional authority by paternalist-frame scholars, structural-exploitation scholars emphasize the concentration of the industry in specific labor market areas, bureaucratic control facilitated by new machinery, technology, and worker segmentation. In addition, changes in the organization of the industry through mergers, consolidations, and plant closings are central themes. Using the structural-exploitation framework, researchers document declining job opportunity, a radically reshaped labor process, and new forms of labor market inequality as firms modernized in their pursuit of new forms and high rates of exploitation (e.g., Bonham 1991; Penn and Leiter 1991; Wood 1986).

The primary strength of the structural-exploitation framework lies in its focus on macro-level processes, such as accumulation. This framework reminds us that southern textile communities have never been completely isolated, either structurally or geographically. The expansion of the industry into the South is part of an historical process of uneven capitalist development that relies on high rates of exploitation and repressive social control. The process continues, although now its scale is worldwide, as markets in labor and commodities have spread throughout the global capitalist system (McMichael 1994; 1996; Stanley 1994).

Structural-exploitation, however, has a number of weaknesses. Researchers using this framework assume that the market structures individual response. They explain human agency as the outcome of market structure. As with other structurally determined models, these explanations diminish attention on the ability of workers to struggle against domination and often fail to articulate the potential of human action, or agency, in the social creation, maintenance, and alteration of structures. Therefore, individuals are viewed as passive objects rather than social actors (e.g., Schulman, Zingraff, Reif 1985; Wood 1986). When structures (be they economic systems, communities, or households) are assumed a priori, researchers produce structurally determinant arguments by conceptualizing inequality as a constant, incapable of erosion (Anderson 1996; Anderson and Roscigno 1995; Anderson and Tomaskovic-Devey 1995).

The structural-exploitation frame suffers from additional shortcomings that are related to the manner in which it interprets modern social change. Mingione notes, "In recent years, sociologists studying economic change have felt an increasing sense of unease which, despite its manifestations, seems to have a common origin, namely, a growing dissatisfaction with the concept of 'development' and the various theoretical paradigms which express it" (1991:1). One reason for the unease is the increased interest in "previously ignored or undervalued" activities, such as informal work, self-provisioning, and a variety of household work strategies that cannot be easily quantified and explained as rational economic behavior. Mingione argues that recent restructuring has resulted in a more "complicated and heterogeneous" labor force (1991:2). As such, the emphasis on market economy disregards the complexity of modern social relations.

In studying the southern textile industry, we need to include social processes in addition to capitalist accumulation in our analyses of mill communities and workplaces. For example, sociologists researching the social consequences of change in southern textiles need to pay adequate attention to the impacts of global change, including international market competition and the global labor supply. In other words, the accumulation process should not be restricted to national boundaries.

To address these shortcomings, researchers using the structural-exploitation framework can incorporate the concept of social relations: the analysis of multiple processes that are historically relevant to the problem at hand. Applied to the structural-exploitation framework, the concept of social relations suggests that we focus on the intertwining processes of social change that influence communities and workplaces.

Summary of Frameworks

Like all theories, the existing frameworks used to explain change in the southern textile industry have both strengths and weaknesses. Paternalism, with its emphasis on workplace and community, offers localized accounts of relations between workers and company owners. By expanding the social context, structural-exploitation provides a means of interpreting change from a global perspective. In this book, I argue it is possible to merge the strengths of both frameworks into an alternative theory of social reproduction that extends beyond cultural and market-determined models.

The alternative framework that will be developed in the text stems from two critical bodies of literature. First, work by Mingione (1991, 1994) on the limitations of the market paradigm calls attention to the importance of informal work activities, heterogeneous patterns of social inequality, and the importance of global linkages. Second, current work on inequality draws attention to the fact that inequality is not one-dimensional, but is a "matrix of domination" (Collins 1990) containing multiple "differences" among race, class, and gender (West and Fernstermaker 1995). Combining new insights from these studies with the strengths from traditional frameworks of paternalism and structural-exploitation, I develop a theory of change based on the concepts of embeddedness and social relations. Recognizing the expansiveness and difficulty of theory construction, however, I narrow the specific focus of this work to the social impacts of global processes on localities. I will analyze change in southern textile communities in the context of embedded social processes. The first step in attempting such an approach is to identify the multiple and interdependent processes that are embedded in both global and local social relations. As will be discussed in the next section, three essential processes operating in our current world economy serve to interconnect the global with the local. These processes are globalization, restructuring, and spatialization.

CONTEMPORARY SOCIAL CHANGE: KEY PROCESSES

In our contemporary era (i.e., post-Fordist, post-modern, post-industrial), several processes have been identified as important in the new global economy. To broaden the usefulness of paternalism and structural-exploitation frameworks, I identify three processes relevant to the current research project. Globalization, restructuring, and spatialization are societal or system-level processes that impact individuals' lives, their options, and the distribution of inequality and opportunity. To understand the social consequences of change in communities and workplaces, we must ask how these processes affect localities. How does the global influence the local?

Globalization, restructuring, and spatialization are interdependent forces operating at the level of the world-system, yet they simultaneously create social consequences for localities. Although the processes are embedded throughout different levels of abstraction and exist in social relationships, for purposes of definition and explication I will consider them separately. Conclusions, however, will be made in light of the fact that the processes do not operate independently of one another. The following paragraphs introduce and apply these concepts to the southern textile industry and raise important research questions for empirical analyses.

Globalization

Although globalization is recognized as an ubiquitous force in the modern world, its meaning is subject to dispute by scholars (Amin and Thrift 1994; McMichael 1994). Generally, globalization is defined as the worldwide integration of economic processes and space (McMichael 1994), an integration that is accompanied by rapid changes in technology and communication. Globalization involves more than just the flow of commodities; it also includes the international movement of labor (Stanley 1994). As McMichael (1994) states, most researchers perceive it as a shift in power from communities and nation-states to international institutions such as transnational corporations, multilateral agencies like international textile associations, and international political organizations (for example, NAFTA and GATT). Unfortunately, this perception suggests that globalization is a homogeneous product formed from a linear political-economic trend rather than resulting from uneven development (McMichael 1994). In addition, the perception overlooks the struggles that occur in local economies and communities (Kanter 1995).

An alternative to conceptualizing globalization as an outcome is to understand it as a formative and contradictory process (see also McMichael 1994). Doing so shifts the focus of research from static outcomes to dynamic patterns of events that may advantage and disadvantage certain members of society, contributing to new geographies of centrality and marginality (Sassen 1994). However, it is recognized that the effects of globalization are distinct in different times and places. Instead of viewing globalization as a universal phenomenon, it is useful to see industries, firms, and households embedded within global economies and seek to understand the impacts of the process at key times and places in history. McMichael (1994) does this by examining the process of capital accumulation as a trans-national project designed to integrate the world.

We currently live in a period of rapid circulation of money, people, goods, ideas, and information. Production and marketing strategies, such as Just-In-Time and Quick Response methods, combined with technological advances in communication, have fundamentally altered the distribution of textile products. Where once it was supply that influenced demand, now large retailers control the requisition of towels and sheets. How do these and other specific forces of globalization impact the United States textile-mill complex and textile-dominated communities? What opportunities and limitations do workers in textile communities face as a consequence of globalization? Posing these questions shifts the focus of research from traditional frames of analysis to macro-change processes and their micro-level consequences, connecting global and local positions. By conceptualizing social phenomena as local-global processes within a specified historical context, we form a basis from which we can begin to analyze the current social consequences of change in southern textile communities.

Restructuring

Restructuring is a term that describes a variety of strategies used by capitalists as they attempt to lower costs and increase profits. For example, company owners may relocate jobs to low-wage areas, or they may de-skill jobs and make the flow of production continuous, decreasing the number of workers needed. Restructuring is encouraged by increased demands that accompany economic globalization, including the need for flexible production, organizational structure, and the use of labor power. As Kennett (1994) explains, restructuring is rooted in regulation theory, or the conceptualization of capitalism as a series of specific stages of accumulation. Scholars debate various aspects of the transition between modern stages of Fordism (linkage of mass production with mass consumption) and post-Fordism (production by continuous flow and semi-automatic assembly lines; consumption facilitated by domestic credit and social welfare). In general, it is assumed that the restructured post-Fordist labor market is responsive to market demands and relies on smaller and less specialized (thus more skilled) labor forces. Standardized mass production, characterized by the use of large-scale workforces on assembly lines, is less evident. In addition, flexibility in management strategy, products, and patterns of consumption are parts of the brave new post-Fordist world (see Piore and Sabel 1984).

Putting the concept of restructuring in two categories is problematic. A post-Fordist analysis would hold that modernization occurred throughout the industry with the advent of flexible specialization. However, as will be shown in the empirical analysis chapters, social reality is not always divisible into such neat categories. Rather, social relations are embedded in historic patterns of social organization resulting in complex, "messy" processes. As will be shown, modernization in textile production has occurred very unevenly. In order to understand the social consequences of change in southern textiles, it is necessary to include the following subject matter: the restructuring of the textile-mill complex, the impact of restructuring on firms and workers, and the degree to which restructuring advantages and/or disadvantages workers. Inquiry into these areas extends our focus on traditional relationships between workers and owners (emphasized in frames of paternalism and structural-exploitation) to include relations among and between firms, industries, and nations, thereby strengthening our understanding of the social impacts of economic change.

Spatialization

Explanations of the social impacts of economic change compel researchers to address spatial unevenness, or the concept that domination and subordination within an industry may vary across time and place. For example, why are some plants within a specific firm unionized while others are not? In addition, what factors explain regional variation in wages? Grant and Wallace (1994) note that the process of spatialization, or employers' heightened use and/or threats of spatial relocation, serves as an important labor-control strategy. They suggest that spatialization occurs in a multitude of forms. Technologically, the process is enhanced by advanced transportation and communication equipment. Organizationally, spatialization occurs using flexible techniques, such as the geographic movement of capital, union avoidance, and job deskilling. Institutionally, spatialization is facilitated by political policies that decrease government centralization and increase power to the states, thereby forcing competition among states. According to Grant and Hutchinson (1996), spatialization has resulted in the general problem of the "shrinking state." They claim that "states are being inserted into a global economy and called upon to play a larger role in deciding their economic destinies, while the forces that shape those destinies are often too overwhelming or distant for [United States] states to manage" (1996:23).

Many aspects of spatialization are evident in the southern textiles industry. Historically, mill owners located plants in the southern United States because it gave them easy access to cotton and an abundant supply of cheap labor. With the establishment of mill villages, company owners controlled the local labor market. Communities depended on the local textile mills for employment. Currently, states such as North Carolina continue to be active in attracting textile plants with offers of tax breaks. One downside of textile-mill dominance over local labor, however, is evident when a mill leaves a community. Workers must find other employment or face poverty. Thus, the process of spatialization (also known as the "spatial fix" according to Harvey 1982) is essential in our understanding of the social impacts of economic change in textile communities.

When linked with the processes of globalization and restructuring, spatialization can improve upon the conclusions drawn from the frameworks of paternalism and structural-exploitation by acknowledging that relationships between dominants and subordinates change over time and place. Specific to the study at hand, key questions include: How has spatialization shaped textile labor markets? What recent trends facilitate spatialization? Moreover, how are workers impacted by spatialization?

An analysis of all three processes is crucial for understanding the social consequences of change in southern textile communities. Conceptualizing them as processes rather than outcomes brings "agency" to the analysis, acknowledging that actors are responsible for social changes. As will be demonstrated in the concluding chapter, placing emphasis on embedded and unequal social relationships strengthens the cultural and market-determined models of paternalism and structural-exploitation.

METHODOLOGY AND ANALYSES: OVERVIEW

So far, I have suggested that the processes of globalization, restructuring, and spatialization are key to understanding the social consequences of change in the southern textile industry. However, social relations among and between the community and the workplace do not exist independently of large-scale social forces, nor are they solely determine by them. Theoretical frameworks that include a focus on processes help us to embed analysis of local impacts in a global context.

The research questions grounded in the processes are indeed multifarious. How are researchers to deal with the multiple and tangled phenomena? This is not an easy question; there is not a firm answer in the textbooks. One common means relies on a division of academic labor, whereby independent researchers focus on one level of abstraction, gathering bits and pieces of information. Sociologists specialize in the study of a single area—the labor market, the firm, the industry, the household, or individual workers, for example. Eventually, somebody might ask each individual scholar for a contribution to an edited anthology. This division of labor, while consistent with the fragmentation of academic disciplines, tends to produce disjointed results. It is rare that the disciplines cross each other's lines (for an exception, see Schulman and Leiter 1991). As Tickamyer (1996) argues, the problem lies in the inadequacies of data conceptualization, production, and collection. Data collected on the industry level will neglect impacts of change at the household level. To address this imbalance, researchers can use a multi-level approach. Multi-level analysis can take different forms, including hierarchical regression analysis (e.g., DiPrete 1990; DiPrete and Grusky 1990), ethnographies (e.g., Fitchen 1995), case studies (e.g., Lee 1995), and extended case studies (e.g., Burawoy 1991). As will be discussed in the next chapter, if these techniques are to be considered multi-leveled, researchers must explicitly collect and analyze data from various layers of social reality.

Applied to an analysis of the social consequences of change in the southern textile industry, a multi-leveled approach needs to integrate the processes with different levels of the social structure, such as the global economy, industry, firm, labor market area, and household. How would one bring about such a multi-leveled approach? I argue that extended case study methodology, offering historically specific explanations that are useful in improving upon existing theories, is one way to start developing a multi-leveled approach. The goal of the extended case is to improve theory by finding failures and rebuilding the theory by referencing wider social forces, including the state, economy, and world system (Burawoy 1991). As will be discussed in Chapter Two, extended case studies provide a structural context for traditional ethnographic analysis.

To incorporate multiple levels, one must view the case not only in terms of geographical boundaries of the site (i.e., the immediate local community of Kannapolis in this study), but as a multiple-layered phenomenon. The case itself is multi-leveled. Levels here can be thought of as horizontal layers representing the organization of structure within the world economy. In turn, processes can be seen as a vertical "twisted braid" (see Myers 1996). For example, globalization, restructuring, and spatialization are processes that cut through the horizontal layers. So to study how the global impacts the local, these processes need to be incorporated into analysis of social change. At certain times, one or more of the processes may be dominant at any given level. However, the important thing to remember in this conceptualization is that neither the levels nor the processes operate independently of one another; each impacts multiple levels of analyses.

A multi-level approach grounds analysis in the principles of embeddedness and social relations and provides a means of substantiating theoretical claims with methodological tools. Research that blends different levels of social reality into nested models is different from research that focuses on a single level in that it allows contingent levels to effect outcomes at other levels. For example, human agency can result in altered structures of production (i.e., strikes can close down production lines). Likewise, structural adjustments can lead to household-level adaptations (i.e., restructuring of work shifts causes parents to find alternative means of childcare).

The strength of a multi-level approach lies in the breadth of analysis it generates and the attention it provides to processes that link layers of abstraction. The data gathered from different layers of social reality provide insight to a number of contexts, including the physical, economic, social, and political. Social phenomena are situational and influenced by happenings of many kinds, requiring that we examine diverse issues and contexts. A multi-level approach allows the researchers to span disciplinary boundaries, integrating theories, methods, concepts, and observations from separate fields of inquiry. For example, as the current research will demonstrate, data on individuals, firms, and industries can be used to inform a study of community and workplace restructuring, illustrating the embeddedness and social relationships among the levels. Such examination provides greater contextual insight into the consequence of workplace restructuring than, for example, a population ecology analysis of the births and deaths of firms in a single industry or an ethnographic study of life in a modern textile town.

Obviously, the massive scope of a multi-level approach has built-in constraints and inherent weaknesses. For example, fieldwork takes longer than secondary data analysis. In addition, the activity associated with multi-level research is equivalent to that of several independent projects with a common literature base. Time, energy, and support (e.g., economic, resource, staff) are essential requirements for multi-level research. Likewise, a multi-level project may sacrifice depth of knowledge for breadth. Researchers must be aware of these potential shortcomings and adjust their findings accordingly.

The present case study includes the community of Kannapolis, North Carolina, and the textile firm, Fieldcrest Cannon, Inc. Given that current social and economic outcomes (e.g., firm downsizing) are influenced by activities in multiple layers, I adopt a multi-level approach in which the household represents a unit for the reproduction of labor power (Schulman and Anderson 1993). The household is embedded in a labor market that has been historically dominated by the one firm, Fieldcrest Cannon. The firm, similarly, is embedded in the United States textile industry and in the international economy. Each of these levels is impacted by a multitude of processes, including globalization, restructuring, and spatialization. Tapping these dimensions requires a multi-level approach.

In Chapter Two, I discuss case study methods. I present strengths and weaknesses of the case studies, along with key research questions, the project reference frame, and data collection techniques. I outline four important levels of analysis for this research project, including the industry, the firm, the labor market, and the household. I will use a set of methods to analyze the levels of social reality within the case. From a historical perspective, I examine the textile industry as a continuum that leads to its current position within the global economy. I consulted existing documents (newspapers, archives, and company literature) and interviewed company executives for the study of the firm. To examine changes in the local labor market area, I relied on secondary data regarding county business patterns. Using semi-structured interviews, I collected data from key informants, including community leaders, community activists, current and former workers, and industry experts. Twenty-seven informants were interviewed, numerous news articles and community specific histories were analyzed, and patterns of demographic change were uncovered with data from United States Census and industry-specific sources.

In addition to detailing the case study and data collection methods, Chapter Two introduces the research site—Fieldcrest Cannon, Inc., located in Kannapolis, North Carolina. Since its founding in 1887 by James W. Cannon, the company has experienced dramatic changes in ownership, production, employment, and management. Likewise, the labor market area has changed, through migration and regional industrial expansion.

I present descriptive analyses of the textile-mill complex and of world and United States patterns of restructuring in Chapters Three and Four. These chapters provide the context for the empirical work, and the bases for hypotheses about the possible outcomes of restructuring. The manufacturing of textiles, either through natural fibers or petro-chemical (human-made) fibers, can be understood as part of a chain that includes multiple linkages. For the present study, the chain is used as a context for understanding change in the textile-mill complex. By textile-mill complex, I mean the part of the chain that takes raw materials and turns them into fabric by carding, combing, spinning, weaving, knitting, and finishing. The specific firm and community under study are involved with home furnishings. Thus, I give special attention to the home furnishings part of the chain. Other parts of the chain, including the supply of raw materials, the apparel end market, the industrial goods end market, and related industries such as textile machinery and chemicals constitute the "context" and will be discussed as they relate to structural adjustments in the textile-mill complex.

I describe the transformation at the firm level, including a history of mergers, cuts in production jobs, modernization, worker resistance, and unionization struggles, in Chapter Five. An essential component in this story is the switch in ownership from family to absentee entrepreneur that shook the 100-year-old paternalistic foundation of social relations in Kannapolis. The new owner, David Murdock, changed work rules, closed plants, sold company housing, and raided the company pension fund. This was not to be the only period of dramatic change for Kannapolis. Four years later, Murdock sold the company to a rival textile firm, Fieldcrest. The merger led to the formation of one of the largest textile firms in the United States, Fieldcrest Cannon. As with most mergers, this change led to more cuts in production jobs.

Following both periods of transformation, workers rallied for unionization. Several campaigns were narrowly defeated, and the National Labor Relations Board has recently charged Fieldcrest Cannon with unfair anti-union tactics. Notwithstanding these charges, restructuring continues, as Fieldcrest Cannon eliminates production jobs with automation. In addition, the firm reorganized its New York operations and relocated the company's division presidents and marketing and operations personnel to Kannapolis. A computer data center opened in 1996 and houses the company's mainframe computers, thereby integrating information-processing and integrating production systems and marketing needs. The centralization and concentration resulting from these changes places Fieldcrest Cannon on a competitive plane with other large retailers who are starting to dominate industry. In addition, the changes leave the community of

Kannapolis, which was once solely dependent on the mills, with significantly fewer textile jobs.

In Chapter Six, I focus on community outcomes. Previous literature suggests that communities that have undergone restructuring as a result of changes in the dominant firm will potentially experience certain social consequences. Outcomes may include a decline in the number of local employment opportunities, increases or decreases in employment opportunities, and new forms of household adaptations and survival strategies. The purpose of this chapter is to demonstrate the degree to which these outcomes exist in the current study.

My analysis of the social consequences of change for the Kannapolis community focuses on three areas—changing labor markets, reconstituted ethnic relations, and household adaptations. The geography of the labor market area under study has changed from 1980 to 1990 and now includes a major metropolitan area—Charlotte, North Carolina—known for international banking, as well as some counties in South Carolina. As a result, commuting and work patterns have changed. People leave Kannapolis to work in other areas. At the same time, people are *moving into* the area to live, a migration that is creating a "bedroom community." In addition, as Hispanics have moved into the community, race relations have changed.

In Kannapolis, recent economic restructuring has led to a decline in real wages, forcing many individuals to work multiple jobs (see also Danziger and Gottschalk 1995; Sklar 1995). Researchers suggest reemployment of textile workers typically means downward mobility; many are unable to get full-time work, and average wages decline (Gaventa and Smith 1991; Penn and Leiter 1991). The degree to which this is true in my case study is contestable, however.

Another potential community outcome is the entrance of new industries into the labor market. Historically, when the Cannon family owned the mills, no other firm was allowed into the unincorporated region. Thus, Cannon tightly controlled the labor pool. With the end of Cannon rule, however, industrialization expanded within the region. Philip Morris, a major cigarette manufacturer, has a plant in the area. Other recent expansions include a prison, a semi-conductor manufacturer, and a poultry plant. As will be discussed, some of these new jobs provide higher wages that textile work. However, the number of ex-textile employees able to obtain such positions is not easily identifiable.

Additional reverberations of change become evident when speaking with workers who work twelve-hour shifts. As will be detailed, the work schedules in some of the continuous-production spinning plants have been modified from three eight-hour shifts to two twelve-hour shifts. Although the schedule alteration is properly a topic related to workplace outcomes, it is also a factor leading to the creation of new household adaptations and survival strategies. The twelve-hour shifts put tremendous strain on families, especially those rearing children. Parents are no longer able to attend children's ball games or volunteer at the schools. Additionally, the grocery bills for some families may escalate with increased reliance on microwave meals. With the decline of the company town, workers have turned to private services for recreation, shopping, banking, and health care. And like always, they rely on each other.

I focus specifically on the workplace in Chapter Seven. Shopfloor changes include the training, skills, and demands of textile jobs. Previous literature suggests that changes in firm and industry structure will impact shopfloor labor processes, bringing about increased production pace, new management strategies, and technological adjustments. The production process is computerized and automated, decreasing the need for workers. How have technological and organizational developments combined to reconfigure the structure and culture of the shopfloor?

The answers that emerge fall into three decisive categories: redefining jobs, teamwork, and unsteady employment. The general automation of the production process has contributed to a decline in the number of workers. Remaining workers are responsible for multiple jobs, as well as subject to increased demands. The company has a new emphasis on teamwork, with modular units—that is, machines and people who are responsible for multiple functions (e.g., hemming, cutting, and sewing)—at their core. Workers are now required to be team players, in contrast to their traditional roles as individuals paid on a piecework basis. Accompanying these changes are problems such as machine breakdowns and unsteady market demand, both of which can result in sporadic employment patterns and unsteady incomes. In Chapter Seven, I conclude that workplace outcomes are embedded in multiple levels. The events taking place on the shopfloor of Fieldcrest Cannon's Kannapolis plants are reflections of the processes of globalization, restructuring, and spatialization.

I summarize the results of the case study in Chapter Eight. I argue that to understand the plight of workers such as the ones in this case study, researchers need to consider various puzzle pieces found at different levels of abstraction. The social impacts of economic change are multi-tiered and are embedded in a local context of class, race, and gender. Levels of analysis, such as the industry, firm, labor market, and household, are not segmented units that exist independent of one another or independent of a context. Rather, they are nested and contingent, rooted in history, geography, and the world economy.

The evidence identifies a set of social relations fraught with contradictions. Globalization, restructuring, and spatialization, which are occurring in a variety of ways, are best understood as processes. The social consequences of change in the community and workplace are embedded in previous sets of social relations. Consequential to societal fragmentation (i.e., Mingione 1991), the processes of change occur unevenly. I conclude

Chapter Eight with an extension of these ideas beyond the specific case, as an attempt to develop a theoretical framework that will integrate previously segmented areas—areas not only within the discipline of sociology, but also areas across different academic boundaries.

Research Methods

In order to understand more fully how macro-level processes such as globalization, spatialization, and restructuring affect the behavior of individuals, we need to apply new research methodologies that incorporate multi-level techniques (Schulman and Anderson 1993). Various agencies (e.g., United States Census Bureau) regularly collect data on numerous social measures. However, it is less easy to catalogue and quantify other social impacts. For example, numerical indicators do not easily elucidate alternative economic activities that may develop importance in communities undergoing change, such as multiple job holdings, unregulated enterprises, home-based work, and self-provisioning (Mingione 1991). These activities are important to people who need immediate income and work-schedule flexibility to accommodate new and multiple roles and responsibilities brought on by changes in the workplace (Mingione 1991). Women and minorities often engage in these activities because they have limited opportunities in formal labor markets. In human terms, when livelihood strategies are limited to formal labor market activities, reduced living standards, deteriorating quality of life, and persistent poverty often result (Mingione 1991). The focus of this book is on the social consequences of global economic restructuring. As such, it is imperative that we investigate social consequences at multiple levels of reality. This chapter explains the methodologies employed.

In the first chapter, I argue toward the development of a new theory based on multi-level research in order to understand the fundamental transformations occurring in textile communities. Multi-level analysis is useful for researchers who desire to blend different layers of social reality into a nested and contingent model. The next question, then, is how are we to bring such a multi-level approach about? According to the current literature, there are two ways.

First, as the work of many social scientists demonstrates, hierarchical linear regression modeling utilizes quantitative data from different levels of analysis. For example, researchers have developed contextual models using trends and cross-sectional data from multiple levels to analyze occupational attainment (DiPrete and Grusky 1990) and fertility (Entwisle and Mason 1985). A second method of operationalizing a multi-level approach uses several qualitative techniques, such as interviews and participant observation, to gather different types of data. Qualitative research techniques such as ethnographies (e.g., Atkinson and Hamersley 1994) and case studies (e.g., Stake 1994) rely on less structured data derived from multiple sources—informants, community records, and observation. Sociologists often extend case studies to political and economic spheres, providing a contextual analysis that may differ from traditional ethnographies (e.g., Burawoy 1991).

I have chosen to use an extended case study in my multi-level approach. The extended case study goes beyond traditional case studies in that it uses both quantitative and qualitative data to examine how the processes of change affect different layers of social organization. The extended case is an especially useful tool for examining the consequences of social change brought by globalization, restructuring, and spatialization to workers and communities because it allows the researcher to obtain data from varying levels—industry, firm, labor market, and household—at which these processes operate.

I begin this chapter with a discussion of the strengths and weaknesses of case studies, citing examples of extended case study research. Next, I explicate the key research questions. A description of the specific research site follows. Finally, I present the data collection techniques used to examine the various levels of the case, including issues of their validity, reliability, and sampling. The chapter concludes with the plan of the analysis.

THE CASE STUDY

In general, there are three types of case studies—intrinsic, instrumental, and collective (Stake 1994). An *intrinsic* case study is undertaken because one wants to better understand a particular person, clinic, curriculum, and so on. The focus of such a study is the object itself. In an *instrumental* case study, researchers examine a particular case only to provide insight into an issue or to refine theory. Here, the object of the study is of secondary interest; it plays a supportive role, facilitating our understanding of something else. While researchers may study the case in depth, the examination occurs only because such detail helps them pursue the external interest. They may or may not view the case as typical of other cases. In an instrumental case study, researchers choose a case because they expect it to advance an understanding of that *other interest* for which the case is a representative example. In the final type of case study, known as a *collective* case study, researchers may examine a number of cases jointly in order to inquire into a phenomenon, population, or general condition of which the cases are parts. For example, a collective case study on the social impacts of global restructuring might include a meta-analysis of individual cases (either intrinsic or instrumental) that cover different research sites (i.e., various industries, communities, or workplaces).

What are the strengths of case studies? Case studies are advantageous research strategies for developing explanatory questions, or those questions that deal with linkages that need to be traced over time. One of the unique strengths of a case study is its ability to deal with a full variety of evidence, including documents, artifacts, interviews, and observations (Yin 1994). Additionally, because case studies involve collecting data in close proximity to a specific situation, they can strengthen confidence since they are affected by "local groundedness," or the influences of local context which are often latent, underlying, or non-obvious (Miles 1994:10). Case studies can also reveal complexity, or the "richness and holism" of a situation (Miles 1994:10). Finally, the fact that researchers collect data over a sustained period makes case studies useful in examining complex processes that may shift over time.

What are the drawbacks of case studies? A common concern about case studies is that they provide little basis for scientific generalization. As Yin (1994) notes, case studies *are* generalizable, but not to populations or universes. Rather, case studies are generalizable to theoretical propositions; thus, they are useful for expanding and generalizing theories, but not for enumerating frequencies or rejecting hypotheses. In addition, case studies may require a great deal of time, especially if detailed, observational evidence is required. They are also difficult to do well. The problem, according to Yin, is that "we have little way of screening or testing for an investigator's ability to do good case studies. People know when they cannot play music; they also know when they cannot do mathematics; and they can be tested for other skills, such as by the bar examination in law. Somehow, the skills for doing good case studies have not yet been defined..." (1994:11).

What can researchers do to addresses the weaknesses of case studies? One way to assure credibility in the case study is to triangulate data. Triangulation is a process that uses multiple perceptions to clarify meaning and to verify the reliability of an observation or interpretation (Denzin 1989). As will be detailed, examples of triangulation include the use of demographic data to back up field reports combined with interviews in which many informants make the same claim independently.

Application of Case Study to Methodology of the Current Project

The research technique I employ is an instrumental case study that envelops multiple levels of social reality. Given that the problem to be addressed—

the social consequences of globalization, restructuring, and spatialization—is not a uni-dimensional or mono-causal phenomenon, we must focus on multiple objects of study, such as the industry (textiles), the firm (Fieldcrest Cannon), and the surrounding community (Kannapolis and its labor market area). Such an approach goes beyond the traditional case study that focuses on a single object of study.

Substantial time on site, personal contact with activities and operations of the case, reflection on the emerging analysis, and revision of interpretations are characteristics of conventional qualitative case studies. Consistent with typical case studies, data for this project were gathered on the nature of the case, its historical background, the physical setting, other contexts (e.g., economic, political, and legal), and on informants through whom the case can be known. In contrast to traditional case studies, however, this project also looks at multiple levels of abstraction (e.g., household, community, and workplace) and employs various research techniques (i.e., statistical, interviewing, and observation) to understand the processes that permeate those levels. Because this research goes beyond the traditional case study (which focuses on a single object of study), it is more appropriate to describe it as an *extended case study* (e.g., Burawoy 1991).

Extended Case Study Exemplars

Extended case studies offer historically specific explanations that are used for constructing and reconstructing theories. The goal of the extended case is to improve theory by finding failures and to rebuild the theory by reference to the effect of broader forces, such as the state, economy, and world system (Burawoy 1991). Theory can fail for a number of reasons, including anomalies, refutation, internal contradictions, and theoretical gaps or silences. The extended case "takes the social situation as the point of empirical examination and works with given general concepts and laws about states, economies, legal orders, and the like to understand how those micro situations are shaped by wider structures" (Burawoy 1991:282). Instead of assuming there is a linear relationship between variables, researchers employing the extended case study assume its elements are indivisibly connected. Analysis is a continual process, mediating between field data and existing theory.

Perhaps the most important difference between extended and traditional case studies is that extended case studies necessitate the examination of political and economic forces. As Burawoy (1991) explains, extended case studies go beyond the traditional limits of participant observation techniques, a method typically limited to an ahistorical period and a micro level of analysis. At the same time, extended case studies provide a structural context for traditional ethnographic analysis. As such, well-executed extended case studies have the potential to address the complex and multi-dimensional problems of social reality.

Various examples of extended case studies exist. I will describe three specifically. First is Lee's (1995) work on gendered production regimes in two factories in the south China manufacturing region. Lee, whose data collection was ethnographic, was a full-time assembly-line worker in two independent electronics factories. At times, she lived in factory dormitories. She also collected data by visiting workers' homes and participating in their weekend activities. Lee's case study put her in a position to appreciate the impact of globalization on the local community. She concluded that in the Asian context, the state is a less important determinant of workers' dependence than are local institutions such as networks, kin, and families. Lee also found that the organization of labor markets explains the varying constrictions of women on the shop floors. As such, gender is a constituent element in class relations that operates through diverse mechanisms. Lee's extended case illustrates that studies of social change must take place on multiple levels and should include examinations of local labor markets, communal networks, the enterprise, and the state. Her work is especially important for sociologists working in the area of gender and transnational corporations undergoing processes of global economic restructuring.

A second example of an extended case study is Lamphere's research of Asian immigrants to the United States (1992; Lamphere and Grenier 1994). By integrating macro-level quantitative data with micro-level qualitative participant observation and intensive interviews, Lamphere connected an ethnographic analysis of the immigrants with an analysis of structure and power, including the shift in the American economy away from manufacturing and towards service industries. Lamphere's extended case studies are notable because the researchers collect data on multiple levels, which provide both a political and economic context for the problems presented, and an analysis of historical trends and patterns of development.

A third key example of extended case study methodology is the work of Beneria and Roldan (1987), who examined the political and economic implications of the increasing concentration of women in the informal sector of the Latin American economy. Literature reviews led them to believe an integrated analysis of class and gender formation, struggle, and recomposition was needed. By critiquing existing definitions of class and gender, they developed an alternative theory of the ways in which class and gender interact in the workplace and household. The researchers' feminist perceptions influenced the interview guide construction, identifying their research as "for" women rather than "on" women. Beneria and Roldan utilized a variety of data collection techniques, including participant observation and formal and informal intensive interviews. These methods allowed them to understand that both the connected impacts of the capital accumulation and the dynamics of the international division of labor influenced changes in the patterns of household interaction and gender subordination. Beneria and Roldan returned to their premise and concluded that both a theoretical and practical redefinition of development is needed, one that incorporates non-economic objectives such as social reproduction.

These studies are examples of extended case research. Each varies in its data collection methods, the amount of time researchers spent in the field, and the degree of participant observation employed. These variations are significant in that they demonstrate the need for theory to guide data collection. In other words, debates about which methods are "best," such as qualitative verses quantitative, should be replaced by an instrumental approach that emphasizes multiple methods selected based on what is appropriate for the question or issue at hand.

We are in the midst of a period of societal transformation, domestically and globally. As social researchers, we need methodology that examines the various processes of transformation at all levels. Tickamyer notes, "while our understanding of the social has been transformed by the reality of events and the expansion of our theoretical horizon, as a discipline we remain tied to the data produced by tired paradigms" (1996:11). It is my intention as a researcher to focus on the processes restructuring our society and examine their impacts on individuals.

DESCRIPTION OF RESEARCH SITE

The firm selected for this extended case study, Fieldcrest Cannon, is especially appropriate for analysis of the social consequences of change in a rural community and workplace brought about by restructuring. Cannon Mills, established in 1887, was a stereotypical paternalistic employer, providing workers with mill housing in the unincorporated town of Kannapolis (Moore and Wingate 1940). In 1982, Cannon family members sold the firm to David H. Murdock. Murdock instituted a set of changes that included altering work rules, closing plants, and raiding the company pension fund (Zingraff 1991). A bitter unionization struggle followed, ending in 1984 with the narrow defeat of the union. Later that same year, Murdock sold his interest in Cannon to Fieldcrest, and the mills in Kannapolis are now part of Fieldcrest Cannon. The number of people employed in the mills has declined from approximately 22,000 in the 1970s to approximately 7,200 in 1994 (U. S. Bureau of the Census, 1996), largely because of changes in technology and labor processes.

Fieldcrest Cannon, based in Eden, North Carolina, designs and produces a wide variety of home textiles, including sheets, blankets, comforters, and towels. Its products are sold to chain stores, department stores, catalog companies, warehouse clubs, home furnishing stores, mass merchants, and, under private labels, to other retail, institutional, government, and contract costumers. In 1993, the firm had eighteen plants located in the Southeast, two of which were in Kannapolis, and several more are in the immediate labor market area. Although close to the metropolitan city of Charlotte, North Carolina, Cabarrus County, in which Kannapolis is located, has a history of limited manufacturing development. As we will see, this is in large part because Cannon Mills controlled the local labor supply and exerted substantial influence on local county politics. Cannon's single-industry hold on the labor market diminished over the years, particularly with the end of family ownership. Currently, although Fieldcrest Cannon is still a key employer in the community, the local labor market has expanded, and new manufacturing industries and jobs have appeared.

Kannapolis, the community surrounding Fieldcrest Cannon, is part of a nine-county labor market area (LMA 009: York, Lancaster, Union, Mecklenburg, Anson, Cabarrus, Chester, Stanly, and Rowan Counties according to the 1990 labor markets geography). Although this labor market has traditionally been highly dependent upon the textile jobs at Cannon Mills, service and other manufacturing industries now dominate the area. As will be discussed, the labor market area has expanded in recent decades to include a major metropolitan area, Charlotte, North Carolina. Workers in the labor market area commute in and out of the towns, providing the region with a flexible labor supply. No longer isolated in a mill village, members of the Kannapolis community interlace an emerging network of employment opportunities.

I selected this specific site for a number of reasons. First, the two-and-one-half hour drive from my research university, North Carolina State University, allowed easy access. Second, I had contacts in the area that offered entry to workers. Third, a decade ago, Kannapolis had the distinction of being the oldest unincorporated town in the nation; remnants of the mill village community, both material and ideological, are still evident. Fourth, the transition from family ownership to corporate buy-out seemed indicative of general patterns within the textile-mill complex in the late 1960s through the early 1980s. And fifth, a series of unionization struggles in the community raised its visibility and attractiveness as a location for the study of social change. Contrary to stereotypes of "docile" southern mill villages, Kannapolis has been and continues to be a site of resistance and negotiation.

DATA COLLECTION TECHNIQUES

My research relies on data collected through a variety of techniques, including historical, statistical, and informant interviewing. The following paragraphs outline the data collection process and explain why each technique was invaluable.

First, I used *historical data* to study the evolution of the textile industry, the selected firm, and the community. As Tuchman argues, "adequate social science includes a theoretical use of historical information. Any social phenomenon must be understood in its historical context" (1994:306). In my particular case, historical data were key to understanding the development of the firm, the mill village that continues to surround the firm, textiles in the southern United States, and the textile-mill complex.

I obtained information from published works addressing these topics, including textile trade journals (e.g., *Textile Outlook International, Textile World*), house publications (*Fieldcrest Cannon Times*), books on community history (e.g., *Weavers of Dreams*), newspaper clippings (e.g., *Charlotte Observer, Kannapolis Daily Independent, Raleigh News and Observer*), and company reports (e.g., *Wall Street Journal*). I used these materials to construct a history of the industry, firm, and community.

The search for historical accounts was aided by the fact that North Carolina State University is home of one of the nation's premier textile schools with an outstanding specialized library, providing easy access to a wealth of information. Additionally, I found local information at the public libraries in Kannapolis and Concord. The multitude of sources and the breadth of information contributed to the saturation of data by reinforcing key pieces of history, thus suggesting reliable data and increasing confidence in the validity of the emergent story.

The second type of data gathered was *statistical*, or secondary quantitative data. Previous research (Lobao 1996; Lobao and Schulman 1991) has shown that the local employment structure, characteristics of the population, geographic location, and farming patterns affect poverty and socioeconomic well-being. The statistical component of my study builds on this work by using county-level data to describe the social, demographic, and economic structure of Kannapolis, Cabarrus County, and the labor market area. These data are important for assessing the socioeconomic impacts of restructuring and for providing a context for subsequent qualitative research.

The central challenge for statistical data gathering lay in delineating the structure of the industry, the composition of the labor force, population characteristics, and household types within the research site. To present such statistical descriptions, I used the Textile and Business Information Systems (TABIS) database, developed by members of the College of Textiles at North Carolina State University. TABIS includes national data from the United States Department of Commerce and Bureau of Census (i.e., population projections by state, age, sex, and race; County Business Pattern summaries containing the number of employees and establishments by SIC), NPA Data Services, Inc. (i.e., key indicators of county growth for 1970-2010; projections for employment, income, earnings per job, number of households, and population by age groups), and the United States Department of Labor, Bureau of Labor Statistics (employment and earning data by SIC). I supplemented this with data from various editions of the City and County database assembled by the United States Census. The majority of the descriptive statistical analyses in this study concentrate on the labor market area (LMA 009).

The third type of data came from *informant interviews*. I used semi-structured interviews to examine the social impacts of restructuring on workers and households. More specifically, informant interviews provided the data to evaluate the extent of labor reorganization within the firm, the historic marginalization of formal labor market involvement, the rise of informal economic activity, support for collective action, and the ways home and work are combined. To generalize findings beyond the individual level, informants were asked to report not just about themselves, but about people like themselves; not just about their personal behavior, but about practices common to their group. This technique generated qualitative, descriptive data that captures household and community level variation, while at the same time instilling trust and assuring respondents of confidentiality.

Appendix One illustrates the interview guide. A large part of the guide is directed at changes in the workplace and community. Given the history of the firm and community, I selected the themes for the guide with the assumption that they would be topics the informants were knowledgeable about and would be willing to discuss. Additional questions, covering such issues as gender and race, were also included in the guide.

To help shape the interview guide and increase its reliability, I conducted a preliminary group interview in October 1993 with approximately eight Kannapolis labor union members (including blacks and whites, women and men, and current and ex-workers). Local organizers of the Amalgamated Clothing and Textile Workers Union (ACTWU), initially contacted through colleagues, introduced me to the group. This interview, which lasted two-and-one-half hours, was relatively unstructured, allowing participants to define issues of importance. Along with a co-facilitator, I probed group members in order to elicit information about changes in the production processes, unionization, gender and race relations, employment opportunities outside of textiles, and impacts of restructuring on households (including childcare and financial responsibilities). The exchange was lively—people talked about their work histories, their current problems, and their adaptations to restructuring. In addition to shaping the interview guide, this group provided me with contacts for further interviews. This initial interview was important for defining research questions, facilitating entry into the community, and establishing contacts for future interviews.

Nine months after the group interview, I made contact with one of the union activists. After explaining the purpose of the study, he agreed to introduce me to other workers. I traveled to Kannapolis twice during this month to meet contacts and set up interviews. All prearranged contacts received an advance letter outlining the purpose of the research (Appendix Two) and a follow-up phone call to confirm meetings. In addition, I acquired several interviews by dropping in on friends of workers, as well as visiting the offices of community leaders.

Obviously, I based the interview strategy on a purposive sample. I benefited from snowball sampling in the pursuit of new leads during fieldwork, being able to take advantage of unexpected possible informants. I relied on a network-interviewing strategy to contact respondents from local community and activist groups (e.g., church, civic clubs, local ACTWU chapter, etc.), and I often dropped in on potential respondents during business hours. I expanded on these networks through door-knocking and by obtaining introductions to friends and neighbors. Additionally, professors at the North Carolina State University College of Textiles facilitated interviews with industry experts. The resulting group of informants varies by race, class, gender, and age, and though not a random sample, represents different social locations within the research site. Groups that stand in different relationships in the textile community have different experiences, concerns, and preferences. For this project, informants are black, white, and Hispanic, women and men, workers, a company executive, community leaders, and textile industry experts.

From the summer of 1994 through the spring of 1996, with the assistance of two colleagues, I conducted interviews with 29 informants (Appendix Three). Typically, we held interviews in the homes of workers and offices of community leaders, social service workers, and economic developers. We held one interview at a secondary work site (the shipping room at a small grocery store); three interviews took place in local restaurants. Interviews averaged one-and-one-half hours, with the longest lasting four hours.

The interviews with textile professors took place on the Centennial Campus of North Carolina State University in Raleigh, North Carolina. A set of interviews with textile workers occurred while touring the plant with two management-level employees. All interviews were recorded in handwritten notes taken during the session, with additional comments appended immediately afterwards. With the exception of one tape-recorded interview that I conducted by myself, a fellow researcher was present for each session. One person would usually take the lead in asking questions and probing while the other diligently took notes. Although we did not record the respondent's voice on tape (with the above exception), this arrangement enabled us to record many direct quotes in the interview notes. Immediately after leaving the interview, the researchers would drive to a neutral location, review notes, and use a tape recorder to detail additional notes and comments. On the same day as the interview, I transcribed the taped summaries and notes into text using a microcomputer, usually with my co-researcher present and contributing to the transcription and reviewing the file for omissions and misrepresentation. In all, we conducted 21 separate interview sessions, covering 29 different individuals (see Appendix Three).

Following the advice of extended case study researchers (e.g., Burawoy 1991), I began analysis as soon as the data were collected, guided by the pre-defined relevant levels (horizontal layers of abstraction), processes (vertical cuts through the levels), and key research questions. The issue-focused analysis included coding (linking what the respondent says with concepts and categories), sorting by major themes (using a computer word processor), and organizing and integrating observations (for further detail on analyses of interview data, see Fontana and Frey 1994; Huberman and Miles 1994; Yin 1993, 1994).

COMBINING MULTIPLE METHODS WITHIN AN EXTENDED CASE STUDY: TRIANGULATION

As described in the previous section, I utilized a variety of data collection techniques in this extended case study. One purpose of employing various methodological procedures is to reduce the likelihood of misinterpretation (Stake 1994). The process of using multiple perceptions to clarify meaning and to verify the reliability of an observation or interpretation is known as triangulation (Denzin 1989). As Huberman and Miles suggest,

> By self-consciously setting out to collect and double-check findings, using multiple sources and modes of evidence, the researcher will build the triangulation process into ongoing data collection. It will be the way he or she got to the finding in the first place—by seeing or hearing multiple instances of it from different sources, using different methods, and by squaring the findings with others with which it should coincide. (1994:438).

Specifically, I rely on the triangulation of historical, statistical, and qualitative methods employed in this extended case study to increase the credibility of my findings. For example, when the research was complete, it was apparent that workers, textile professors, and company executives used similar descriptions of the impacts of global economic restructuring of the textile-mill complex. (This is not to imply, however, that their interpretations about the social impacts of these changes were in harmony.) Likewise, changes specific to the firm of Fieldcrest Cannon (identified through interviews with workers, managers, and executives) mirrored general restructuring trends in the United States textile-mill complex (ascertained by industry literature and interviews with textile professors). Evidence of a final example lies in the fact that the historical data supported the accounts of community life provided by workers, as well as their description of changes in labor market employment patterns. In each instance, the overlap of historical, statistical, and interview data reinforced the validity of findings.

In addition to providing triangulation of data, the multi-level approach enables the researcher to link layers of abstraction. The data gathered from different layers of social reality provide insight to a number of contexts, including the physical, economic, social, and political. Researchers can use data on individuals, firms, and industries to inform a future study on community and workplace restructuring, illuminating the embeddedness within and social relationships between levels of analysis. Such examination provides greater contextual insight to community and workplace outcomes than perusal utilizing single-method procedure.

JUSTIFICATION AND ETHICAL CONCERNS

The field research techniques used in this study are common in small-scale, focused research projects and ethnographies (e.g., Erlandson et al. 1993; Fitchen 1991, 1994, 1995; Fontana and Frey 1994; Jackson 1987; Lofland 1971; Spradley 1979; Taylor and Bogdan 1984). Use of semi-structured interviewing requires the researcher to guide the interview by a set of basic questions and issues to be explored, but neither the exact wording nor the order of questions is predetermined (Erlandson et al. 1993). Semi-structured interviewing provides greater breadth and depth of data than standard questionnaire interviewing (Fontana and Frey 1994). Semi-structured interviews help the researcher to understand and put into a larger context the interpersonal, social and cultural aspects of the environment (Erlandson et al. 1993). In keeping with such parameters, the interviewing techniques I use in this study were flexible and dynamic, with the goal of understanding informants' perspectives on their lives, experiences, and situations as expressed in their own words. For all cases, I attempted to conduct the interviews as a conversation between equals, rather than a formal question-and-answer exchange (Taylor and Bogdan 1984).

The key to getting rich data from dialogue is in asking good questions and in careful listening and recording. While it is important to prepare a list of carefully worded questions that reflect the basic research question and problem of the study, the researcher must be careful not to be bound or overly structured by those questions and must allow them to emerge naturally over the course of the interview (Erlandson et al. 1993). Thus, the researcher enters the interview with a well-organized plan, built around the central questions and issues. While the researcher may have a written interview guide to consult, it is imperative that the guide is indelibly printed in her/his mind (Erlandson et al. 1993). The guide is not a structured schedule or protocol. Rather, the researcher uses it as a reminder of general areas to cover with each informant. As a social researcher, it is important to take advantage of a situation when the respondent spontaneously addresses a scheduled but unasked question. The researcher should utilize a respondent's spontaneity, considering it an asset rather than an intrusion to be stifled in an attempt to keep the interview on track. Researchers are then responsible for asking appropriate follow-up questions to obtain additional needed information in the new area resulting from spontaneous interaction.

The logic of semi-structured interviewing is that information elicited early in the interview helps define the subsequent line of questioning that researchers pursue. The use of new information to focus subsequent attention is the hallmark of semi-structured interviewing. When well conducted, such interviews sound, to the casual listener, like a frank conversation about a limited range of topics (Merton, Fiske, and Kendall 1990). Semi-structured interviews allow people to narrate their own lives and emphasize what seems most meaningful and important to them. Researchers design the interviews to allow conversation to flow freely, to a certain extent. The interviewer raises questions and topics for conversation, but within that structure, respondents are free to talk as much or as little as they chose and free to deviate from the topic at hand. Thus, respondents will have some control over the content of their interviews. This style of interviewing provides information that is not specifically asked for but that may be helpful in understanding the individual and her or his work.

Given that a variety of informants were to be interviewed in this extended case study, each with different experiences, backgrounds, and knowledge, I developed several different interview guides, building each one around the experiences and knowledge of the respondent. For example, the interviews with current workers tended to emphasize changes in the labor process, focusing on the respondents' descriptions of various aspects of work, family, and community tasks and relationships. Specific questions were included to address working conditions such as pay, hours, schedules, and household survival strategies. In contrast, the interviews with community leaders focused on key problems in the community, such as job skills, training, and future development. The reader will find basic interview guides in Appendix One.

As noted, I obtained field contacts through a variety of sources, ranging from local union members to economic developers to textile professors. Contacts led to co-workers, friends, relatives, or neighbors. Searching for an initial contact was often time-consuming and trying. For example, workers on twelve-hour shifts had little free time to talk, so it was difficult for me to find an available respondent under these conditions. Additionally, access to key minority groups was initially limited; I did not gain entry to the booming Hispanic community until the final stage of research.

I contacted all potential respondents via a letter of introduction (Appendix Two), by phone (including the ones I dropped in on), or both. I explained the purpose of the research and asked to schedule a time to meet. While the majority of scheduled interviews met as planned, several did not. I assume this was because the respondent forgot, had a sudden conflict, or simply decided against the interview. Upon meeting with respondents, I asked them to sign the informed consent mandated by University Human Subjects Guidelines, ensuring that the results would be confidential and anonymous.

I decided not to use a tape recorder based on several factors. First, given the explosive history of labor unrest, which, according to Stone and Heffner (1995) is generally repressed, I assumed that textile workers in the community might be reluctant to have their voices recorded. In the preliminary interview, members had discussed the community's fear of labor unrest and had warned that many people would be adverse to interview requests. Indeed, numerous contacts refused to even talk with us on the topic. Typically, the refusals took the form of polite excuses and missed appointments. Justifications ranged from being out of town for several months to anticipating an organ transplant (either kidney or lung, the respondent was not sure which it would be). In two cases, the respondents told me that they simply did not want to talk.

I conducted the interviews in a manner that reflected ethical concerns, addressing issues of consent, deception, privacy, harm, identification and confidentiality, trust, and betrayal. Given the company's previous and recent labor-law violations, the fear expressed by workers is understandable. I was well aware that association with the research project might unfairly cause a worker to lose his/her job at the mill. A researcher's presence in the community is a potential cause of emotional pain and interpersonal stress (Fontana and Frey 1994). One must be mindful of ethical considerations when entering a community, maintaining confidentiality and protecting sources. In this study, I protect respondents by disguising their identity in order to limit the risk that findings could be used against them.

In addition to ethical concerns, other reasons exist for the interviewing strategy. For example, tape-recording interviews may introduce biases, including potential complications that may ensue in the interview situation and the social deference behavior that tends to arise with the use of a tape recorder. Discretely taking field notes on paper and immediately transcribing them afterwards is a well-developed tradition in the social sciences (see Emerson 1981; Erlandson et al. 1993; Gordon 1980; Lofland 1971; Taylor and Bogdan 1984; Webb et al. 1966). As noted by Jackson,

> The data collection technology that gives the collector the best opportunity to observe what's going on, the best chance to understand the broad interrelation of things and events, the greatest physical mobility, and the least cost, is probably a sharp eye and a good memory. Next is paper and pen. All machines must be corrected or altered to operate in changing physical conditions; pen and paper work anywhere...[while they may] generally bring back the least amount of detail, that doesn't mean the detail they bring back is the least important or the least useful. (1987:111).

More important than the manner in which field notes are recorded is the need for regular note-taking and prompt, frequent analysis (Fontana and Frey 1994; Lofland 1971).

In sum, not tape-recording the interviews served several purposes. First, it allowed access to respondents who otherwise may not have talked with me. Second, it reassured respondents of the confidentiality of my research. And third, it forced the interviewers to pay strict attention and work as a team in order to record data. Obviously, there are weaknesses in this technique. Even with two researchers present, it is likely that we omitted some data because of memory limitations. Additionally, there were times when my co-researchers and I did not agree on specific details. Overall, however, the decision not to tape interviews was in the best interest of the research project given the history of fear and repression that surrounds southern mill villages.

CONCLUSION: PLAN OF ANALYSIS

Any method of research has biases, strengths, and weaknesses. I will discuss these at length in the concluding chapter. This research uses many data sources and methods of data collection to increase the opportunity for triangulation of valid data and to aid interpretation. The use of several interviewers provided multiple perceptions to clarify meanings and interpretations. The various methods tapped different dimensions, including work- and community-based phenomena, and were appropriate, given the breadth of the project.

Thus, in this study, the extended case employed various data collection methods, including historical, statistical, and informant interviewing. The data were coded, sorted, and organized around the key processes identified in the literature review (globalization, restructuring, and spatialization) and analyzed according to two emergent categories: outcomes for the community and outcomes for the workplace. The next two chapters provide information about the context for the case study, including an overview of the global textile industry and the United States textile-mill complex. Chapter Five uses the historical materials to provide a social history of the firm. Chapters Six and Seven use the quantitative and the qualitative data to analyze social consequences in the community and workplace. Chapter Eight summarizes the results, presents some tentative answers to the key research questions, and develops a new theoretical framework for the analysis of social consequences.

Understanding Globalization through World Patterns of Change in Textiles
Building International Social Relationships

In previous chapters, I presented the foundation for an extended case study framework to analyze the social impacts of change in a southern textile community. I argued that researchers must address relevant processes, such as globalization, restructuring, and spatialization, using a multi-level approach in order to understand complex social relationships and the structures within which they are embedded. The first step in developing such an analysis involves examining the context in which these processes occur. What follows is a description of major trends in the world textile economy and the adjustments that firms in the United States textile-mill complex have made in reaction to these trends.

Beginning in the 1950s and accelerating from the early 1970s to the present, there have been significant modifications in the global textile industry. These changes have occurred within a world system created by the United States in the aftermath of World War II when the infrastructure for a global economy was put into place (e.g., the Bretton Woods agreements and the International Monetary Fund). Two key periods can be noted: first, the *development project* was initiated as a strategy for improving the condition of the Third World (see McMichael 1996). During this phase, nations attempted to initiate a variety of forms of industrial development to emulate the patterns that had unfolded in the West. When the resulting global production began to threaten firms in the United States and other dominant countries, these powerful nation-states stepped in to regulate economic growth by implementing worldwide trade and monetary structures such as the North American Free Trade Association (NAFTA) and the Asia-Pacific Economic Conference (APEC). The succeeding debt crisis and the development of multinational corporations signaled a new phase, the *globalization project*, where production for export, international sourcing, and global commodity chains became dominant. The shift from development within individual nation-states to a globalized system that influenced production and market demand resulted in a rapid escalation in the scale and international operations of larger companies, as well as the technical reorganization of production in developed countries (McMichael 1996).

From a world-system approach, the textile industry exemplifies the industrialization process in regions of Europe and the United States. Similarly, as other countries moved toward economic development, the textile sector played a vital role in industrialization efforts. Today, virtually every country in the world produces at least some textile products (Dickerson 1995). In many ways, the stages of development in textile production parallel the overall development of countries or regions. For example, the number of textile-producer nations has increased dramatically because Third World countries use textile production to begin industrialization. Additionally, many of the developing countries (e.g., Taiwan) that first established textile production have become more proficient producers than countries with existing textile production. This is because the new textile mills are capable of manufacturing products with increased technical expertise, precision, and efficiency. Finally, whereas manufacturers in the developed countries have depended primarily on their own home markets for growth, producers in the developing countries look to exports for growth. These factors contribute to a growing global system to supply the consumers of the world, one that results in an extremely competitive global market (Dickerson 1995).

In order to understand how globalization creates impacts on the local level, it is important to identify and understand the general changes that have affected the United States textile industry. The next section contains a historical overview of the world textile industry, noting the policies that have specifically affected textile production and distribution in the United States. Key questions I will address in this chapter include: What are the major trends and changes in the global textile system in the past century? How does the global system affect the United States textile-mill complex? Who are the key players in the global textile system? The supply and demand dynamics of the textile market shift as developing countries enter the global competition. As will be evident, the globalization project has resulted in new challenges for the textile firms and textile-producing countries whose dominance of the market was previously unassailable.

GLOBALIZATION AND TEXTILES

According to Dickerson (1995), the textile industry entered global relations in the 1950s as a growing number of producer nations emerged and as the world economy in general became more global. During the 1960s, developing countries substantially increased their share of global production, and their growth rates far outpaced those in the developed countries. Today, the global textile system links all textile firms. To understand the global context, the following section focuses on the development of the global textile economy in the post-World War II era.

Global Textile Economy

By the late 1800s and the early 1900s, growing threats to economic nationalism emerged as powerful countries claimed new lands as sources of raw materials. Nations concerned with protecting markets from imports began imposing tariffs, quotas, and other restrictions. The two World Wars and the Great Depression negatively affected international cooperation. Nationalistic economic policies, such as tariffs, trade restrictions, and devalued currencies, slowed global trade (Dickerson 1995).

The leadership of major trading countries, including the United States, England, and Germany, tried to keep their domestic markets protected during the start of the development project. To mitigate the potential negative consequences of increased global trade, the countries initiated two early post-war efforts. First, in 1944, representatives of the Allied governments met in Bretton Woods, New Hampshire, and established the International Monetary Fund (IMF) to stabilize international monetary exchange. Second, in 1947, the General Agreement on Tariffs and Trade (GATT) was established to promote unrestricted trade, particularly by the reduction of tariffs. The founding principle of GATT was its "most favored nation" provision, which meant that if a country gives a trade advantage to one country, it should give the same advantage to every other country with whom it trades. Thus, every country would have an equal opportunity in trade with another. However, unique provisions were included for the textile and apparel trade that permitted countries to violate this principle.

The United States textile industry prospered during the first 25 years of GATT's existence. As one of the few major industrial economies not damaged by World War II, the United States was in an advantageous position of being able to produce textiles for exportation. However, by 1955, Japan had developed a new and productive textile complex and was rapidly expanding its exports of cotton fabric and apparel to the United States. Japan joined GATT in 1955 and agreed to voluntarily limit cotton fabric and blouse exports to the United States (Cline 1987; Dickerson 1995).

Restricting imports from one country provided room for other countries to enter the competition for dominant markets such as those in the United States, England, and Germany (Aggarwal 1985). For example, Hong Kong, which did not have the same general market dependence on the United States and thus could not be influenced to adopt voluntary export restriction pressures, responded rapidly to fill the gap in the United States market created by the restriction on Japan's textile products.

By the 1960s, the textile and apparel industries in most industrialized countries felt the impact of increased imports from the low-wage developing countries. Many newly developing countries had begun producing textiles. The output of rebuilt textile sectors in industrialized nations after World War II combined with production from the new entries accounted for a sevenfold increase in international textile production between 1945 and 1975 (Ford 1986). Virtually all of the roughly 200 nations in the world now produce textile products, and most of them produce at least some of those products for world markets (Dickerson 1995). The textile sectors of industrialized countries were unable to offset the influx of imports with a comparable increase in exports. To further complicate the problem, the world market grew minimally during the 1970s, and political leaders often blamed the trade imbalances for unemployment, plant closings, and decreased company profits (Dickerson 1995).

In 1960, President John Kennedy wanted to help expand world trade, but recognized the political importance of exempting United States cotton textile and apparel trade from GATT rules (Dickerson 1995). Kennedy's sensitivity to the United States textile industry was no doubt the result of the tremendous number of textile constituents and their representatives from key states (Dickerson 1995). Kennedy proposed a seven-point program to assist United States firms. One of the points directed the State Department to hold a conference of textile importing and exporting countries to develop an international agreement that would govern the textile trade.

As a result, temporary country-by-country quotas by country were established under the Short Term Arrangement (STA) until a long-term solution to trade imbalances could be developed. Thus, in 1961, the STA created a new set of trade rules for textiles and apparel alongside the existing rules of GATT. Representatives from key nation-states, such as the United States, Germany, and England, treated the textiles industry as a "special case" because of the political significance of textiles to their countries. These dominant bodies made a case for special provisions. They argued that the low start-up costs of textile production would unfairly enhance new countries' market shares and diminish the outcome of production in existing textile-dominant countries, thereby threatening the global economic activity (Cline 1987).

In February 1962, the Long Term Arrangement Regarding Cotton Textiles (LTA), an agreement among nineteen major trading nations that was to be effective for a period of five years, replaced the STA. The LTA covered only cotton—wool and manufactured fibers were to remain under industry control. Like the STA, the LTA was an exception to GATT rules. Under its conditions, importing countries could negotiate bilateral agreements controlling the trade of cotton products. The LTA permitted importing countries to restrain imports of cotton textiles from low-wage countries. Once a supplier was brought under restrictions, its exports were allowed only slow growth from year to year. The LTA was renewed in 1967 and again in 1970 (Cline 1987).

By 1973, 82 countries had signed the LTA and participated in textile trade under its policies. The next step was the Arrangement Regarding International Trade in Textiles, more commonly known as the Multifiber Arrangement (MFA), which extended the provisions of the LTA to wool and manufacturing fibers. The MFA was a response in part to the impact of bilateral agreements the United States made with Japan, Hong Kong, and Korea since 1971. Because of these bilateral agreements, growing quantities of Asian textile goods were diverted from the American market and were imported to European markets. European Community members began pressuring for protection from imports originally destined for the United States (Dickerson 1995). Leaders of the global economy recognized it was time for a larger, more coordinated solution to world textile trade. The MFA became effective in January 1974 for a four-year period. It was renegotiated in the years between 1977 and 1993 with extensions and appended changes to the original MFA. The result was a total of four MFAs and three extensions. (For further explanation of the MFA extensions, see Dickerson 1995).

The MFA represents an attempt to mediate the different positions of exporting countries and importing countries. In general, few participants have been satisfied (Dickerson 1995). Exporting countries believe the restrictions are too harsh, while importing countries find them overly lenient. As a result, leaders have negotiated various additional agreements. Two major Multilateral Trade Negotiations (MTNs) (the Kennedy Round and the Tokyo Round) provided special concessions to most textile and apparel products. Exporting countries continued to express frustrations over growing restrictions on their textile and apparel products. In 1986, the Uruguay Round was launched with the goal of bringing textile and apparel trade back under normal GATT rules. In December 1993, at a continuation of the Uruguay Round, the contracting parties of GATT agreed to plans to phase out the MFA over a ten-year period. (For a discussion of the Uruguay Round of multilateral trade negotiations, see Hamilton 1990 and Schott 1994.) Finally, another landmark in global trade, the North American Free Trade Agreement (NAFTA) was affected January 1, 1994, in which Canada, Mexico, and the United States entered a free trade agreement. (For an overview of issues and prospects of NAFTA, see McConnell and MacPherson 1994.)

Policies such as GATT and NAFTA are not pertinent solely to textiles. Indeed, these policies affect the production of numerous other commodities. Because the process of globalization has resulted in uneven capitalist development and the implementation of the globalization project occurs at varying rates, policies that are effective in controlling trade imbalances in one commodity are not necessarily effective for another. In fact, such policies can contribute to the uneven development of nations and industries. For textiles, this has meant that some countries have rapidly developed high-tech textile production that exceeds the existing standards of traditional manufacturing nations.

As noted above, the growth of efficient overseas production has resulted in a series of state interventions to regulate trade, especially in apparel (see, for example, Toyne et al. 1984), but also in textiles (e.g., STA, LTA, MFA). Next, we need to turn our attention to the shift from the development project to the globalization project, a shift that has serious economic implications for the world textile trade and one whose global entanglements, in turn, influence local communities. For example, as nations impose trade restrictions, firms often close and relocate production plants. In many cases, the social impacts can be devastating for individual workers, their households, and communities.

Globalization of Production

To this point, my discussion of globalization has concentrated upon world trade policies, with an emphasis on regulations that control importing and exporting. What has the implementation of such policies meant to United States textiles? Specifically, how have firms in the textile-mill complex responded to them? Perhaps the most notable response is that United States firms have not increased large-scale exporting. In contrast to the apparel industry, United States textile firms have had a poor export performance over the years (Dickerson 1995; *Economic Intelligence Unit* 1992). In general, United States textile executives have maintained an aversion to overseas business and to dealing with foreign and local governments and banking institutions. Rules and regulations associated with such transactions are cumbersome and usually require experience and languages other than English.

Additionally, as long as a large domestic market was readily available to United States producers, there was little economic incentive to pursue business overseas. During difficult market periods, however, United States firms would increase efforts to sell overseas. Once local demand returned to normal patterns, United States firms would curtail their efforts. As a result, the United States has appeared as a non-reliable and non-committal supplier of yarns and fabrics, leaving many overseas customers looking to the United States for spot orders only (*Economic Intelligence Unit* 1992). Because United States textile firms have not demonstrated commitment to overseas consumers, repeat business is rare. United States firms often give foreign contracts second priority relative to local customers' orders. Many international trade strategies have failed as overseas customers recognize that United States firms treat them as second-class customers. These customers often refuse to enter serious trading relationships for fear of abandonment (*Textile Outlook International* 1994).

According to a magazine interview with James Fitzgibbons, past president of the American Textile Manufacturers Institute and past CEO of

Fieldcrest Cannon, another reason that United States textile firms refrain from international trade is the costs of shipping. During the time when he was CEO, Fieldcrest Cannon sold its products in 60 countries, accounting for less than 8% of sales. As Fitzgibbons said,

> I don't think all of the tapping [of emerging international markets] is going to be done with products exported from the United States because it's expensive to ship halfway around the world. I know that Gillette doesn't ship razors from Boston to every other country in the world, although they sell them everywhere. They make them regionally, and that's going to happen to textiles as well (*Textile World*, March 1996:35).

While globalization has not increased the amount of textile goods exported by United States firms, in general it has been responsible for an increase in export-import trade across other nation-state boundaries. More important, however, is the impact globalization has had on the production process. For example, many countries maintain production facilities for products such as automobiles, computers, toys, and clothing in locations throughout the world. As such, globalization influences not just the flow of commodities across nation-state boundaries, but also the international competition of workers throughout the world economy (Stanley 1994). Because of the increased competition stemming from the internationalization of capital and labor, capitalists have gained the ability to reduce their labor costs substantially and to demand concessions from communities and nations. As will be discussed in detail in the next chapter, the globalization project has increased the ability of powerful firms to relocate jobs, instigating a "global smokestack chase" (Grant and Hutchinson 1996).

During the time developed countries were facing an increase in imports that competed with locally developed products, they were also shifting their manufacturing base to other, less developed countries, a process known as deindustrialization (Bluestone and Harrison 1982). The shift from the development to the globalization project was accompanied by the rise of transnational corporations (TNCs), global firms that are able to use advanced communications and transportation technology to coordinate manufacturing in multiple locations simultaneously. TNCs can be powerful—decisions made solely based on profit and motivated by a desire to influence trade policies can potentially impact individual nations as well as the global economy (Bonacich and Waller 1994).

Although the production of textiles can be found in most countries, not all have the conditions necessary to support an entire textile-mill complex. For example, not all countries have the land or climate necessary for the production of agricultural products such as cotton and wool. Additionally, textile production is capital- and technology-intensive and thus requires the organizational environments found in industrial countries (Cline 1987).

Some less industrialized countries do not have the technological or financial capabilities to develop and support the chemical complexes required to produce manufactured fibers or textile machinery. Others lack the necessary internal markets required to achieve economies of scale in the production of manufactured fibers. As a result, there is considerable variation among countries in their capacity to maintain local textile manufacturing industries, their dependence upon foreign inputs and/or markets, and their abilities to compete internationally.

Beginning with the post-World War II era of the development project and extending to the globalization project of today, the entry of third world exports into the United States has engendered major changes in the United States textile-mill complex (Economic Intelligence Unit 1992). Many Asian countries (e.g., Japan, Hong Kong, Taiwan and South Korea) already support world-class or near world-class industries that rely on exports for survival. China is also in the process of developing a modern textile industry. These developments, combined with the conversion of the East European countries into market-oriented economies, result in more intense global competition (Economic Intelligence Unit 1992).

Specifically, how has globalization impacted the production process in the textile-mill complex? The primarily evidence of its effects can be found in the establishment of foreign-owned plants in the United States. Since the 1980s, foreign entrepreneurs have been attracted to United States textile manufacturers due to the large United States market and the relative stability and predictability of the United States social, political, and economic institutions. For the most part, foreign owners purchasing controlling interests in ongoing United States operations come from Canada, Japan, the United Kingdom, Italy, and France. Other countries represented include Germany, Israel, China, Austria, Hong Kong, Denmark, Morocco, South Korea, and Thailand (Economic Intelligence Unit 1992). For example, the Takata Corporation of Japan owns the industrial fabric division of Burlington Industries. The Hong Kong firm Tal Apparel, Ltd., owns another branch of Burlington Industries located in Ramseur, North Carolina, that makes synthetic and blended yarns and fabrics (Dickerson 1995).

Some textile firms that are owned by parent firms in other countries relocate to the southeast United States, where cheap and unorganized labor is abundant. For example, during 1987 alone, 51 companies from other countries, mostly in textiles and apparel, moved or expanded operations in South Carolina (Standard & Poor's 1988). Among the countries that have made significant United States textile investments are Korea, France, Germany, Switzerland, and Japan. The European Union has also experienced this trend; for example, Japan's textile giant, Toray, built one of Europe's largest textile facilities in England (Dickerson 1995).

Although one would expect to see the process of globalization on United States textile firms evidenced by a corresponding interest in ownership of foreign plants, that has not been the case. According to a 1992 Economic Intelligence Unit Special Report, United States textile firms rarely pursue ownership of textile operations overseas. In the past, some large vertically integrated companies such as Burlington Industries, Cannon, and Springs Industries have owned textile operations overseas, but these ventures have been unsuccessful and eventually abandoned. Two reasons might explain this: one, there is not a large enough market, and two, the cost of shipping products from international sites is higher than the cost of domestic labor. Relative to this particular case, Cannon's efforts to establish a household products business for European markets from a Republic of Ireland base in the late 1970s was discontinued when it became clear that plant operations were oversized for the market potential and that products were not in tune with European standards of construction and content (informant interview; *Economic Intelligence Unit* 1992).

In addition, some United States and foreign textile firms have gone global on a limited basis through transnational corporations (TNCs), direct investment, or joint ownership. For example, Hoeschst, a large German multinational chemical firm, secured the United States fiber division of Celenase, creating Hoeschst-Celenase. Both Hoeschst-Celenase and the United States fiber producer DuPont have established manufacturing plants in regions outside their home countries, providing access to additional markets for the company's products. DuPont supposedly spent $1 billion in the 1990s to build nylon plants in Asia to assure its position in a region where consumption is growing at twice the world average rate (Economic Intelligence Unit 1992).

Another TNC is Coats Viyella, a large, broadly diversified textile and apparel firm based in the United Kingdom. Coats Viyella produces yarns, threads, fabrics, trims, zippers, apparel, and textile home furnishings. This TNC has operations in countries throughout Europe, North American, South America, Asia, Africa, and Australia (Dickerson 1995). Finally, Sara Lee has purchased hosiery companies in other countries, such as Mexico, Italy, and France. The company has built its own production and distribution facilities in other countries as part of its worldwide expansion plan, a move that not only enables it to sell the products of the acquired company, but also provides access to those markets for Sara Lee's own brands (Dickerson 1995).

An additional change that has the potential to impact the United States textile-mill complex is outsourcing, the process through which certain aspects of the production of goods is contracted to an unrelated vendor whose facilities and labor supply are often remote. Today, a great amount of outsourcing of apparel takes place overseas, primarily in the Caribbean Basin and along the Mexican-United States border (Textile Outlook International 1994). Firms are drawn to politically stable countries where supplies of low-cost labor are plentiful. As a result, United States production of goods declines. However, outsourcing has less of an impact on the home furnishing end-market of the textile-mill complex than for apparel and industrial goods because the production of items such as sheets, pillowcases, and towels allows the use of "non-manufacturing technology" or computer-driven production. Unlike the complexities involved in sewing a shirtsleeve or collar, straight-lined textile products can be hemmed automatically. As such, home furnishing products require little, if any, finishing.

In sum, the globalization of the United States textile-mill complex is embedded in the world economy and international trade policies. Global industrial expansion has the potential to play a significant role in the transformation of the United States textile-mill complex, including production, sourcing, importing, and exporting. Although many of these opportunities have not been fully pursued by firms in the United States textile-mill complex, and many are restricted by current trade policies, they nonetheless remain important contingencies. Given the embeddedness of the textile-mill complex in the globalization project, it is imperative that researchers remain attuned to the social relationships between the United States textile-mill complex and the global system.

CONCLUSION

Firms in the United States textile-mill complex are embedded in a world system. International competition has strengthened, and other suppliers of textile products challenge the United States textile industry. Modern geographical boundaries are less important than previously, as potential markets (suppliers and retailers) have become international. It is true that the United States textile-mill complex is not *pro-active* in pursuing non-United States markets, suppliers, or overseas expansion. However, globalization effects are *acting upon* the United States textile-mill complex and changing the context of action. The embeddedness of United States firms in the globalization project subjects them to international forces, regardless of demonstrations of (or lack of) agency.

In the past, the firms in the United States textile-mill complex dominated end markets, controlled production, and regulated supply. Today, increased global competition has provided retailers and suppliers more control over production. As new firms and countries enter the global market, the international balance between supply and demand shifts. Firms may turn to the state for increased regulation when they can no longer dominate the market. When the supply of producers increases and the demand for products remains constant, dominant firms may face increased competition from new firms offering alternative solutions. As such, no single firm or nation can take market dominance for granted.

In summary, changes in the world economy since World War II, including new markets, fresh supplies of labor and raw materials, and contemporary world policies, directly impact the United States textile-mill complex. The relational field of the United States textile-mill complex includes new players—international firms that compete in the finite textile products market. As will be discussed in the concluding chapter, the emerging field also includes new winners and new losers. These relationships are not limited to macro levels of abstraction; social impacts of the embedded process of globalization appear on local levels, affecting both firms and communities. In the next chapter, I begin to link globalization with local outcomes by focusing on national level restructuring in United States textiles. Global influences will be extended in Chapter Five by focusing on the history of a specific community and workplace. In Chapters Six and Seven, analysis of specific outcomes will demonstrate the linkage of global-local processes within a specific southern textile community.

Chapter Four

Understanding Restructuring through National Patterns of Change in Textiles
Strengthening United States Manufacturing

Economic pressures compel textile firm owners to change their scale and methods of production. National and international in origin, these pressures include competition from other firms, shifts in demand, and changes in technology. Capitalists can respond to them in a variety of ways. Firm owners can intensify production without changing technology (i.e., speeding up assembly lines), they can introduce technical changes in production, or they can rationalize existing capacity (i.e., downsizing, closing plants, etc.) As Massey and Meegan (1985) argue, general employment change is the outcome of many hundreds of economic pressures, each specific to their point in history, specific to individual firms and industries, and each pushing and pulling in different directions.

The 1970s and 1980s were critical transition years for firms in the United States textile-mill complex; the rise of international competition and new technology was forcing the industry through a profound transformation. Firms were experiencing changes on all fronts—in the types of products produced, the organization of production and marketing, the structure, scale, and scope of the enterprises producing them, and in the nature of jobs created directly and indirectly by the industry. United States manufacturers were forced to change their production strategies in order to remain competitive at the global level. Textile firms began to increase production in the hope that economies of scale would help them retain their competitiveness (Angel 1994). However, as the firms grew larger, production became less flexible, and they were less able to respond to changing retailer and consumer demands. In addition, the economies of scale were not able to offset the wage advantages offered by developing countries. Both production and employment in the United States textile mill-complex declined (Dickerson 1995).

Today, the worldwide realignments of capital and labor brought about by the globalization project continue to exert profound pressures on firms.

Previous research suggests that the industry has responded with a shift toward consumer/retailer-driven production, more automated machinery, advanced technology, corporate mergers, and growth in the share of foreign-owned or -controlled textile companies. Consequently, textile firms have witnessed declines in number, decreases in employment, and a new sexual division of labor (Johnson 1990; Penn and Leiter 1991; Gaventa and Smith 1991). We can consider these responses as part of the process of restructuring. In this chapter, I will present and illustrate the restructuring process as it relates to the United States textile-mill complex.

RESTRUCTURING

While there is little consensus on what restructuring entails, social researchers generally understand the process to be a continual feature of economic development (Taplin and Winterton 1996). For purposes of my research, restructuring is a global economic management strategy that results in the reorganization of social, economic, and political institutions. Like globalization, *the process of restructuring manifests itself differently in varying contexts and results in diverse outcomes.*

Restructuring occurs in different ways at multiple levels. At the firm level, traditional restructuring includes the reorganization of the labor process resulting from the introduction of new technology, increasing the pace of work, and heightening supervisory control. At the industry level, however, restructuring takes the form of capital concentration through mergers that eliminate or incorporate weaker competitors. At the global level, restructuring creates impacts on wage relations along national lines. Also known as downward leveling, the process involves reducing national wages towards the minimum standard, typically found in the less industrialized, lower-cost regions (McMichael 1996).

Restructuring is of particular importance to sociologists seeking to understand the social consequences of change. For example, one of the most significant results of restructuring in the United States textile-mill complex is the decline in employment opportunities. As firms modernize, close, and merge, they also displace workers. Because mill jobs in the southern United States have tended to dominate many local labor markets, ex-textile employees in these areas may find few alternative job opportunities. Consequently, community members can expect economic hardships. However, to understand the social consequences of restructuring, we first need to know the forms restructuring takes in the United States textile-mill complex. In this chapter, I present examples including technological innovations, market-driven production, and firm downsizing.

Restructuring Effected by Technological Developments

Restructuring can occur as firms invest in equipment and new technology (Castells and Henderson 1987). In large part, the increased mechanization resulting from the introduction of advanced machinery has led to productivity increases and reduced job opportunities. In the last 50 years, there has been an explosion in machinery and process technology. Virtually every textile process has been reshaped and improved in the name of efficiency. Open-ended spinning, shuttleless looms, increased fiber polymer extrusion rates, wider looms, and robotics for in-plant transit are examples of technical change that have "modernized" the industry and increased the pace of production (Dickerson 1995). These developments have fundamentally changed the way companies manufacture products, manage operations, and serve customers.

The major developments in textile machinery have been influenced by the need to achieve lower costs per product unit, greater control over machines and products, elimination of process steps, integrated sequential processing systems based on modular combination, and electronic high tech maintenance (Textile Outlook International 1990). Textile production, now integrated and computer driven, relies more on computerized machinery and less on human labor.

Before the advent of computers and microprocessors, simple mechanical, hydraulic, and electrical assemblies controlled and monitored textile machines. These machines could only be preset for such functions as speed, time, and dimension. Other variables were not monitored or controlled. For example, early machines might stop in the event of yarn breakage, but they could not account for any physical changes in the materials being processed. Factors such as moisture and temperature, which vary continually and affect product quality, were not monitored. In mass production manufacturing, little attention was paid to the quality and properties of intermediate steps. Later, online-process-control-measuring equipment was introduced, with the goal of establishing standards at each production stage, thus ensuring that a product proceeding to the next manufacturing station met required operating and performance standards (Dickerson 1995; Economic Intelligence Unit 1992; plant tour 1996).

Early modernization and technical developments concentrated on the automation of individual machines and retrofitting external controls to existing machinery. Over time, textile machine builders incorporated these controls as an integral part of the manufacturing unit. Interlinking steps in operations such as yarn spinning followed (Economic Intelligence Unit 1992). Interlinking reduces the number of steps in the production process. One example is the changeover to faster and more productive shuttleless looms used in weaving. The use of shuttleless looms, which employ a variety of technologies such as air jets, water jets, rigid or flexible rapiers, or projectiles to insert the weft, has been one of the most significant changes in machinery, facilitating faster and more efficient production and thereby decreasing the need for human labor (Textile Outlook International 1996).

Textile machinery has also become increasingly programmable, incorporating greater diagnostic capabilities to detect and display the location and cause of mechanical and electrical problems and thereby promoting more continuous processing (Economic Intelligence Unit 1992). Reflecting the impact of the technological change is the statement of one company executive in a semi-structured interview: "We're removing the non-value-added steps. We're linking the machines so we don't have to have a person whose job is simply to take something off one machine and put it on another." Production becomes more efficient. Higher speed machines and more controlled operating conditions have resulted in increased productivity.

Technological developments have progressed to the point where the concept of a fully automated textile-mill complex—one that requires no human labor—is possible. Experts predict that textile mills will soon become highly automated, "lights-out" plants (Dickerson 1995; Finnie 1990; informant interview). According to these predictions, the mill of the future will be a series of modular manufacturing systems, each consisting of electronically and mechanically connected components linked to each other through communication networks, to enable mostly labor-free and cost-effective operations within modules. Weaving, for example, will be unattended, and workers will not have to be on hand to take care of doffing (removal of full roving cans). Currently, although some labor-free modules now exist (e.g., yarn spinning), only selected machinery and process technology have advanced sufficiently to the point they could be used in the automated mill of the future (*Economic Intelligence Unit* 1992; Finnie 1990).

Restructuring is premised on flexible work techniques that separate the conception of work from its execution (Castells 1985; Grant and Hutchinson 1996). The installation of more technologically sophisticated, less labor-intensive equipment has resulted in increased total textile production. In the last decade, the textile industry has dedicated a significant amount of money ($2 billion per year) toward investments to upgrade production (Standard and Poor's 1992). That investment notwithstanding, restructuring via technology occurs unevenly and is affected by other factors that may keep the fully automated textile mill from becoming reality. At this stage, manufacturers concentrate on improving individual machines and small process steps, making little progress toward the increased coordination of production units.

The lack of standardization of computers and software used by various machine builders and textile companies compounds the problem of coordinating the various aspects of the production process. Textile executives are still acquiring new technology for their firms; however, they continue to justify capital investments as they have since the 1950s—purely on the basis that improved technological equipment lowers production costs. They have paid little attention to marketplace issues and rapidly changing consumer needs (Finnie 1990). In other words, owners are purchasing new equipment with a short-term mentality and are struggling to keep up with the latest technology. Machines continue to be inflexible and inevitably become obsolete.

We can speculate that the high costs of overhauling an entire textile plant restrict most owners from undertaking a complete renovation. It is very possible that only the most powerful (i.e., market dominant) firms will be able to continue to purchase upgrades that allow them to remain competitive in the global market. In addition, one might argue that because the United States textile-mill complex has been relatively protected and isolated from global competition (see previous chapter), owners may experience a false sense of security. Most likely, as capitalists, owners of textile firms adhere to a short-term mentality of "quick fixes" and are not interested in large outlays for future development (Grant and Hutchinson 1996).

Restructuring via Consumer-Driven Production

Firms within the United States textile-mill complex spent over $8 billion in the five years between 1987 and 1992 modernizing and adopting state-of-the-art processing and communications technology (Economic Intelligence Unit 1992). In addition, quick-response (QR), Just-In-Time (JIT), and "Crafted with Pride" programs (campaigns that encourage United States shoppers to buy American products) are further attempts by domestic manufacturers to retain and recapture business, which in some cases had already shifted to overseas sources. Many of these programs reflect another major change in the textile-mill complex: the shift toward retail or consumer-driven production.

Historically, the United States textile-mill complex has been production-driven. Largely, firm owners controlled the rate of production, the products, and the prices. Interviews and historical accounts illustrate the significance of this for textile firms. For example, under former mill owner Charles Cannon (1921-1971), who was known for creating and maintaining an average of one job for one additional person each day for 50 years, production at Cannon Mills did not stop for anything, not even the depression of the 1930s. Cannon had brick warehouses built and used them to stock surplus goods, and the mills ran continuously.

United States textile firms remained production-driven for the next several decades, benefiting from a captured market of consumers with few alternatives. By the 1960s, however, imported fabrics had grown, and many customers, especially in apparel, turned to overseas producers for variety and lower costs (Finnie 1990). As discussed in the previous chapter, globalization led to greater alternatives for consumers and increased competition among firms for market dominance. At this time, the supply of textile goods reached and exceeded demand.

What were United States firms to do now? One response was to realign production retail needs. The point of consumer-driven production was to coordinate all stages of the distribution chain in an effort to reduce delivery times (Economic Intelligence Unit 1992). Driven by large retailers, firms such as Fieldcrest Cannon utilized JIT and QR production, waiting for retailers to place orders before producing goods. Fieldcrest Cannon chief executive officer James Fitzgibbons and other company executives describe how customers such as Wal-Mart, Kmart, and Target transmit orders on Sunday night. The company must ship by Thursday, or the retailer would cancel the order (*Textile World*, March 1996; plant tour and interview by researcher). Strategies such as JIT and QR shorten delivery times and provide other efficiencies in the production and market chain, and retailers are then encouraged to buy from domestic manufacturers because they can deliver products quickly and as needed.

In order to meet the pressures of such demands, the many independent segments of the textile-mill complex must work closely together. This requires good communication among fiber, textile, and retail operations. Through computer linkages, each segment responds promptly with the merchandise needed by the end-use customer. The computer linkage system transmits point-of-sale (POS) information through the successive stages of the complex. For example, through use of computerized registers (i.e., universal product coding), retailers can capture at the point of sale detailed information on towels sold (vendor, style, size, color). Retailers communicate the information to manufacturers, who replenish stock by providing more towels of the same color and style. The linkages may extend as far back as the fiber producers. In short, the computer linkages set in motion automatic replenishment, or just-in-time responses. Space and distance are no longer barriers between manufacturers and retailers.

Restructuring via Downsizing and Ownership Changes

One current result of restructuring in the textile industry is rationalization of existing firms and facilities in order to establish fewer, more efficient producers and a number of specialized companies (Dickerson 1995). Mergers, leveraged buyouts, and increased diversification are examples of efforts to streamline company operations and make production more efficient and cost effective (see also Finnie 1990). Since 1973, downsizing—a reduction in the labor force—has also been a major form of adjustment used by United States firms in the textile-mill complex. The revitalization of outmoded and inefficient plants can accompany downsizing. As plants become increasingly automated, fewer employees are needed, and in fact, numerous plants simply cease operations. For example, more than 350 textile plants in the United States were closed between 1981 and 1986

(Standard and Poor's 1987). Between 1972 and 1985, the government documented a loss of 700,000 textile jobs in the United States. As Census figures attest, the total number of employees in textile firms has declined dramatically, from 885,000 in 1979 to 717,000 in 1982, to 691,000 in 1990 and down to 671,000 in 1992 (United States Census of Manufacturing 1992). Officials project another 100,000 decrease by the year 2005, dropping the number of textile mill employees to 571,000 (United States Census of Manufacturing 1992). The 22 percent decrease in employment is evidence of smaller, less worker-intensive firms.

The incidence of changes of ownership in the last few years has been unprecedented, as companies have striven to improve competitiveness and gain market position (Finnie 1990). These changes represent another structural adjustment occurring in the textile-mill complex. In the United States, the latter part of the 1980s was a period of merger mania. Mergers enable companies to provide a larger capital base and thereby invest in the modernization programs required to maintain competitiveness of the United States textile-mill complex. Additionally, mergers can potentially result in increased economies of scale and monopolistic control of markets.

We can classify acquisitions such as mergers and takeovers in the textile-mill complex into several categories. First, the owner of one textile company can take over another textile company. Often, the additional production facilities strengthen the original firm by giving it the capacity to target desired niches or increase market dominance. Examples of such acquisitions include Fieldcrest's buyout of Cannon Mills in 1986; Springs Industries' acquisition of M. Lowenstein in 1985; and Mount Bernon's purchase of Riegel Textiles in 1986 (Economic Intelligence Unit 1992).

Second, outside investors can use leveraged buyouts (LBOs) for entry. In the late 1980s, some major publicly held textile companies whose common stock was under-priced relative to asset values were attractive targets for outside entrepreneurs. These new owners, who were both domestic and foreign-based, speculated that they could reduce operating costs and improve price/earnings ratios. That, in turn, would escalate stock prices sufficiently to yield attractive capital gains on their original investments. Often in an LBO, securities will be issued to finance purchases that are backed by the target corporation's assets. In the 1980s, junk bonds and the willingness of financial institutions to use leveraged buyouts accelerated fierce investor activity. For example, Odyssey Partners, Drexel Burnham Lambert, and a private investor, James Ammeen, formerly of Burlington Industries, undertook the formation of Forstmann and Company (Economic Intelligence Unit 1992). The Wickes Company bought Collins and Aikman in 1986; Wesray Capital bought New River Industries in 1989; and Schick International acquired Reeves Brothers in 1986. Another example, the subject of this case study, will be discussed at length in the next chapter—David Murdock's acquisition of Cannon Mills.

In addition to ownership changes, major companies have exited the industry. During the 1980-1981 recession, Crompton and Company declared bankruptcy, and thus the largest corduroy and velvet fabric producer in the United States was eliminated from competition in these specialized markets. Its failure also showed that concentration and specialization on only two product lines did not guarantee business success. It is worth noting that Crompton was probably the only major United States textile company totally committed to an international marketing strategy to sell to and service overseas markets with dedication (*Economic Intelligence Unit* 1992).

There have been many other plant closures, particularly in 1989 and 1990. Today, there are even fewer textile companies. As county business patterns documents, the number of textile establishments has dropped from 6,630 in 1982 to 6,412 in 1987, and further to 6,133 in 1992, resulting in a corresponding 22% decrease in employment (United States Census of Manufacturing 1996). The process of restructuring, as evidenced by the introduction of flexible work techniques, relocation of firms, and changes in ownership, has shaken the previously stable industry. To survive, textile company owners must face reorganization. One industry source suggests the possibility that junk bonds will be credited as the catalyst that enabled companies to reorganize and adapt to the changing world (*Economic Intelligence Unit* 1992).

CONCLUSION

It is important to understand the United States textile-mill complex as an organization embedded in a global system. The previous chapter discussed the global-trade context. This chapter focused on the effect of restructuring, particularly on the United States textile-mill complex. As shown, retail restructuring, including the shift to consumer-driven production (i.e., QR and JIT strategies) and changes in corporation ownership (i.e., mergers, buyouts, and plant closings) have altered the structure and operations of the United States textile-mill complex. As a result, the machinery and technology that underlie production continue to be transformed. In addition, the relocation and downsizing of textile plants adds a geographical dimension to structural adjustments.

Why is the restructuring of the textile-mill complex important to the specific research at hand? As will become evident in the next chapter, the particular firm under study reflects many facets of this process. Both the firm and community are embedded in a history of mergers, downsizing, and modernization. These changes are not necessarily linear or causal; rather they exist as social relations within the firm, and they link the firm to the textile-mill complex and global industry. In the next chapter, I illustrate another key process, spatialization, and focus on the social history of the case study textile firm, Fieldcrest Cannon, Inc.

Understanding Spatialization through Company Corporate History
The Remaking of Community and Workplace Control

In the previous two chapters, I described important changes in the world economy, the world textile industry, and the United States textile-mill complex, including the expansion of the globalization project, technological developments in textile production, and changes in the ownership of textile firms. These events have significant impacts for textile workers and their communities. Researchers can understand the impacts, which are specific to historical and geographical contexts, by examining the process of spatialization. As defined in Chapter One, at a general level, spatialization refers to the assumption that social relations and social processes vary across time and place.

Southern textiles have always had a spatial dimension, defined by the interaction between community and workplace. For example, theories of paternalism typically demonstrate the spatial aspect by the existence of one-industry towns and mill housing (e.g., Freeze 1991; Newman 1978). In contrast, researchers within the structural-exploitation framework demonstrate spatialization by regional relocation (Wood 1986), race and gender composition of employment (Johnson 1990; Penn and Leiter 1991), or deindustrialization (Gaventa and Smith 1991). Although the theoretical assumptions of each frame differ, both associate impacts of economic change with a spatial redistribution of jobs.

The process of spatialization unites the competing frames by drawing attention to the relationship between structure and agency; more specifically, spatialization provides a means of linking local social impacts with global economic forces (Massey and Meegan 1979; Sassen 1990). For this extended case study, the spatialization process centers on the firm and community integration, embedding local outcomes in the larger context of industry transition. Therefore, to understand the local aspects of southern textiles, I will trace the history of the case study firm, Fieldcrest Cannon, Inc., and its mill community of Kannapolis using secondary historical and primary interview data. The historical analysis suggests three key periods of the organization of the firm and the local community. The first period is almost a century long, from the late 1800s to 1982, when the Cannon family governed the firm and the community. A leveraged buyout of the firm by David Murdock and transition in the community marks the second period, 1982 to 1986. The merger of Cannon Mills with its key rival, Fieldcrest, Inc., and the incorporation of the community characterize the period from 1986 to 1997. These periods are important to the case because they represent different forms of community and workplace integration.

PHASE I: THE CANNON FAMILY MILLS

The history of textile firms in the South is the history of families—the families that owned the local mills and the families that labored in them. As previously discussed, mills were typically located in rural areas, and the company dominated the town, controlling the political, social, and economic spheres of activity. Cannon Mills exemplifies the paternalistic southern textile firm and community: a company town, family owners, and struggling mill workers. As will be shown, owners controlled the production process with vertical integration, and they controlled workers through workplace and community power structures. Owner power in the locality was reinforced by conditions of the labor market, the workers' economic dependence, and their lack of geographical mobility. The first period, characterized by family ownership of Cannon Mills from the late 1800s to 1982, illustrates how paternalism, workplace efficiency, and worker control are combined in both the workplace and the community.

In the late 1800s, when the economy of the Carolinas was suffering from the impact of the Civil War, thousands of people were jobless; others survived on small farms. During this time, a massive social crusade was led by the "pioneer capitalists of the New South Piedmont," establishing what would become a tradition of business and manufacturing success for families such as Duke, Cannon, and Gray (Tullos 1989). These powerful landed families had dominated southern society and politics during the antebellum period and were key players in the building of the industrial "New South" (Billings 1990). For example, cotton planters recognized that textile production could be a means of industrial diversification as well as a strategy to counter New England's domination of the manufacturing of goods (Billings 1979, 1982; Zingraff 1991). The relocation of textile production to the South provided opportunities for elite landowners to become capitalist entrepreneurs. Prominent cotton planters, who were also key political figures, built cotton mills in the South (Bartley 1983; Billings 1979; Escott 1985). Under the guise of saving impoverished white farmers, these planters/mill owners provided jobs and offered local markets for agriculture, thus initiating their control over the production and marketing of textiles.

One of the industrial leaders in North Carolina was James William Cannon. Like other southern businesspersons, he questioned why southern farmers had to sell cotton at five cents a pound and buy finished goods at 20 or 25 cents a yard (Young 1963). Intrigued with the textile business and the idea of developing an economic alternative to the distribution system, Cannon raised $75,000 and began a small yarn spinning plant in Concord, North Carolina in 1894 (Ely and Larkin 1987). Cannon could purchase machinery, cotton, and labor locally. Like other mill owners, he recruited white sharecroppers to work as mill hands (Hall et al. 1987). Cannon, following a tradition of racism, gained white workers' loyalty by a guarantee of jobs for whites only. Cannon's strategies of using local materials and providing opportunities for white workers in the rural South provided perhaps the start of a paternalistic system of control that would come to benefit Cannon Mills for the next century.

James Cannon centralized the production process that broke the established pattern of segmented production. He installed everything under one roof—cards, looms, and the other machinery that transformed cotton into the final product, sheeting. Previously, southern farmers sent their cotton to the north for basic fabric production. In addition, Cannon restructured the production process by vertical integration, a top-down method that provided him with greater control over workers and over the local community. Another method of control during this era was the introduction of time clocks. Workers came into factories and labored according to owner-instated schedules rather than schedules reflecting the demands of local markets or regional growing seasons. Under Cannon, control over production resided with the capitalist, not with the worker. The efficiency of the production process increased, but unlike during the era of craftwork and subsistence farming, the mill workers' lives were void of autonomy and decision-making power (Schor 1992).

In addition to technological and organizational innovations, Cannon introduced a number of business techniques that distinguished his company from other textile mills. Instead of selling fabric simply as cotton cloth, James Cannon put his name on it, reasoning that customers who liked the product would ask for it by name, thereby increasing demand (Ely and Larkin 1987). The popularity of "Cannon Cloth" spread throughout the South, validating the Cannon retailing philosophy (Collins 1994). Later, James Cannon sought other markets by producing items in addition to sheets. He saw an opportunity in the increased use of towels by the middle-class and aimed sales at this market. At the time, upper-income consumers used linen towels, and those with lower incomes used flower sacks or other cheap cloth (Young 1963). In Concord, Cannon expanded his towel manufacturing plant, which produced cotton huck (flat weave) towels, and in 1898, he opened another mill that produced cotton terry towels. The reasonable prices of these products made them attractive to both middle- and lower-class consumers. Cannon Mills expanded again in 1908 with the opening of new production facilities that featured automatic terry looms, an innovation that enabled the production of more towels than any other group of mills (Collins 1994). Additionally, with arrival of power lines from the Southern Power Company (now known as Duke Power), Cannon converted from steam power to electricity. By 1914, Cannon Mills had earned the distinction of being the largest manufacturer of towels in the United States.

Efficient production of towels was not James Cannon's only goal—historians note his aspirations of building a model textile city around the industrial plant (Moore and Wingate 1940). Cannon purchased a 600-acre parcel of land, previously a cotton plantation, and began developing a community around the mill that became Kannapolis. Local historians claim the name is a combination of two Greek words meaning "city of looms" (Ely and Larkin 1987).

The development of a local mill village was to have significant consequences for workers and their families. In addition to providing the spatial unification for a reorganized production process, Kannapolis became a stereotypical paternalistic textile-mill community, borrowing and enhancing the early forms of control found on southern plantations. Cannon, as the primary investor, controlled the development of the town. From 1905 to 1910, James Cannon bought farmland around the mills and spent thousands of dollars (in the form of donations, loans, and gifts) to build mills, houses, churches, stores, schools, and banks. He recruited workers from nearby farms and leased white-painted clapboard houses to them for living quarters. The houses surrounded the mill in a circle, facilitating travel to work and close supervision at all times. Cannon had a large lake constructed as part of expansive recreation facilities (Young 1963). He went on to later fund the beginnings of the police department, post office, theater, YMCA, railway station, and a highway to span the nine miles between Kannapolis and Concord. The division of power in the mills was reflected in the spatial division of the two localities—workers lived in the unincorporated town of Kannapolis, while owners and managers lived in Concord, the county seat.

The life and culture of the mill community upheld the traditional relationship between workers and owners that was evidenced on early plantations (see also Billings 1990; McLaurin 1971). The mill employed multiple members of the family, including children (Hall et al. 1987). The family wage system was in effect, meaning that men received higher wages on the assumption that they needed to provide for the family (Hall et al. 1987; Penn and Leiter 1991). Women and children, working equally long and hard hours, received significantly lower wages. White workers dominated production jobs until the 1960s; black workers, if any, worked as janitors or in the bale-opening room (Blauner 1964; Schulman, Zingraff, and Reif

1985). In addition to reinforcing class, gender, and racial divisions, the family nature of labor was an outgrowth of the paternalism of owners and, in turn, provided them with greater control over workers.

Cannon continued to operate vertically integrated plants in spatially segregated communities, and in 1916 introduced a marketing innovation that extended control of the products all the way to the marketplace. Cannon began selling its goods through its own sales organization, Cannon Mills, Inc., established in New York City. This was in stark contrast to other textile manufacturers who sold through commissioned merchants and other independent textile sales organizations (Ely and Larkin 1987). At Cannon, bales of cotton were brought into one door of the plant, and carloads of finished products were sent out another. But Cannon control did not stop there—Cannon salespeople, who were responsible for getting sheets and towels to wholesale and retail dealers, went directly into stores and showed merchants how to sell Cannon towels to what they considered the ideal consumer, the "American housewife" (Moore and Wingate 1940).

That Cannon was eminently successful is evidenced not only by the development of facilities and the growth of Kannapolis, but also by its expansion to plants in China Grove, Albemarle, Concord, and Salisbury in North Carolina, and additional mills in South Carolina, Georgia, and Alabama (Young 1963). James Cannon died in 1921, at which time he controlled 12 mills with over 15,000 employees, more than 600,000 spindles and 10,000 looms, and an estimated $40 million in annual sales (Collins 1994; Young 1963).

After the death of James W. Cannon, his son, Charles Albert Cannon, became the company president. Charles Cannon had been "reared to be a textile man," with the "clatter of looms in his ears, and the excitement of buying and selling in his brain, and he couldn't wait to get into the business" (Young 1963:41). Before his father's death, the younger Cannon had acquired significant experience in the business. At the age of 19, he quit college to start work in his father's mills; he was named manager of the Barringer Manufacturing Company, a small spinning mill in Rockwell, North Carolina, and at 23 years of age, he was elected vice-president of the Cannon Manufacturing Company at Kannapolis (Young 1963). The ability of the Cannon family to pass executive offices to sons coincided with the continuation of previous patterns of paternalistic social relations. Mill workers did not have to adjust to a "new" owner; rather, family tradition ensured the smooth passage of company and community control.

Charles Cannon took office the year after the textile depression of 1920. Industry-wide worker strife marked this era for southern textile workers (Hall et al. 1987). Labor shortages, especially during World War I, had given workers some degree of power and autonomy. In 1920, however, the textile industry declined, as markets dwindled. Many southern mill owners reacted by cutting wages, going on short-time (i.e., cutting back hours), imposing stretch-outs (i.e., piece rates fall, equipment speed increases, and managers assign workers additional machines), and closing plants (Zingraff 1991). At the same time, cotton and tobacco prices began to fall, and more farmers left their land in search of mill employment. The convergence of these two phenomena left southern textile owners with a surplus labor supply and minimal turnover. Mill owners took advantage of the situation and began reorganizing production and enforcing stricter labor controls (Simon 1991).

Initially, workers accepted wage reductions because the cost of living was also falling in a general postwar deflation (Hall et al. 1987). Eventually, workers complained about the harsher controls placed over the pace of their work. Some southern workers belonged to local unions and pressured the United Textile Workers Union (UTW) to call a region-wide strike. However, the UTW lacked funds and did not believe a victory was likely in the midst of an industry-wide depression. Leaders initially encouraged workers to negotiate with their employers. However, North Carolina and South Carolina millhands were adamant (Hall et al. 1987). The UTW, fearing a possible defection of southern loyalists, called a strike on June 1, 1921 at Chadwick-Hoskins and Highland Park Mills in Charlotte and at Cannon Mills in Concord and Kannapolis. Approximately 9,000 workers supported the insurgency. Union leaders chose these particular mills because they were "out after the big fellows...knew these Charlotte and Concord boys had been through this thing before and they would stick to the fight once they were out" (quoted in Hall et al. 1987:191).

The 1921 strikes in Concord and Charlotte began with solidarity—the affected mills were 85-90 percent organized (Hall et al. 1987). However, few families could stay out indefinitely. At the outset of the strike, workers had waived their right to union benefits. Although the UTW attempted to provide minimal support, millhands became discontent over the lack of food. A back-to-work movement began August 11, 1921 at Locke Mills in Concord. Strike sympathizers jeered returning workers, but by this time, the strikers' resources were exhausted. The real turning point came on August 15, 1921, when the state militia arrived in Concord and forced the reopening of the remaining mills. The governor of North Carolina, Cameron Morrison, was a conservative with close family and professional ties to the Piedmont business elite. Although Morrison would not meet with striking workers, he was quick to comply when Charles Cannon requested troops. There was no compromise or negotiation. As Hall et al. report, the presence of the military overwhelmed the union, and "quietly, efficiently, ruthlessly, the union was blotted out" (1987:195). Thus paternalistic control, combined with the repressive power of the state, ensured the continuation of Cannon's power over mill production and workers' lives.

Charles Cannon ran the company for the next 50 years. Cannon Mills maintained its dominant position in the United States towel market, regularly producing half of all towels purchased. During these years, the success of Cannon Mills was due to a combination of technologically efficient production practices and a tradition of worker deference created by decades of paternalistic control. Moreover, as discussed, the firm led the industry by vertically integrating all aspects of textile manufacturing, from the spinning of the cotton to the finished product.

The spatial distribution of plants and communities is an example of the structural embeddedness of tight production control. For example, all the mills were located within a 20-mile radius of one another, and the CEO's office was located only a few steps away from Plant Number 1. This geography afforded extremely close supervision that also had a reach far beyond the confines of the plant. One interview respondent stated that Cannon would dismiss workers for fighting or drinking, even if it happened out of town. Under Cannon, one interview respondent, an ex-mill employee, claimed Kannapolis was a "one-horse town with two rear ends" where Charles Cannon was the "daddy of the town."

Another illustration of the structural embeddedness of paternalist control was the fact that Kannapolis was an unincorporated town. As such, it had no mayor, town council, or legal charter. Cannon Mills paid for the community's police and fire services and was responsible for its water and sewage system, trash collection, and street maintenance. The company owned approximately 1,600 houses that it rented to mill employees, and Cannon owned virtually all the property within the one-square-mile business district (Collins 1994). Described by a community leader informant as a "benevolent dictator," Cannon would not allow any other industry into the area.

The Cannon name grew not only in the community, but also in the market. In 1923, Charles Cannon extended his father's use of the family name to label its products by developing a trademark that would also be sewn into the towels. Once again, Cannon was the first company to use this method of advertising. The trademark featured an antique artillery field piece—a howitzer—that was a mainstay of the Civil War artillery regiments. Cannon used it to symbolize a business that was to "emerge successfully from the shambles of the Reconstruction Era" (Ely and Larkin 1987). Charles Cannon continued the national consumer advertising program initiated by his father to sell Cannon products, developing an intense brand loyalty among consumers. Unlike other companies, Cannon used its name on both top-of-the-line goods as well as more affordably priced items, increasing the pool of customers by tapping a range of incomes (Collins 1994).

In 1927, Charles Cannon brought his textile business to the New York Stock Exchange, becoming the first southern mill owner to do so. The following year, 1928, he consolidated the mills into a single entity, officially named Cannon Mills Company, with headquarters established in Kannapolis. At the reorganization meeting, it was no surprise that stockholders elected Charles Cannon president of the company. Cannon expanded production, which to this point concentrated on towels, and entered the sheet manufacturing business in 1929. For many years, Charles Cannon resisted turning out anything but white sheets. Textile competitors described him as shrewd and fiscally conservative, making no effort to diversify (Collins 1994). Instead, he rode the wave of industrialization and enjoyed the benefits of a firm with market dominance. Rather than responding to consumer demand, Cannon controlled it.

The depression of the 1930s did not close Cannon Mills. Plants continued to operate on a limited basis in spite of poor business. Cannon built numerous brick warehouses and used them to store unsold goods. Profits dropped to a low of $500,000, but the company never showed a loss (Ely and Larkin 1987). Why was Cannon able to continue production? The answer lies in the unintended consequences of industry-wide labor unrest.

Across the nation, textile workers were again disgruntled over losing control of the pace of their work and lives. As Zingraff (1991) reports, these issues exploded in 1929, several months before the Great Depression, with a worker revolt in Elizabethton, Tennessee. The insurgency flowed into central North Carolina, to the towns of Gastonia and Marion. Gastonia gained national attention for its Communist party leadership, along with the shooting deaths of a sheriff and a union balladeer (Pope 1942). Marion was noted for the lawlessness of its deputies who shot into a crowd, wounding 25 and killing 6 (Hall et al. 1987; Zingraff 1991).

These events laid the groundwork for the General Strike of 1934, organized by the United Textile Workers (UTW). Within a few weeks, approximately four hundred thousand workers left the mills, virtually closing down the industry (Zingraff 1991). How did workers overcome the spatial isolation of company towns? Historical accounts point to "flying squadrons" of workers going from town to town, daily radio talks, and traveling musicians singing of labor organizing. Thus, despite residing in spatially isolated company towns, workers were able to mobilize.

One unintended consequence, however, was that with numerous workers on strike, mills such as Cannon were able to continue production *during the depression* in part because they did not have to support a large labor force—the strike reduced the labor force during the depression. (The workers who remained on the job did not necessarily oppose the strike. Rather, many did not feel they could abandon the financial support their jobs provided.) Thus, the General Strike of 1934 actually helped enable continued production in some plants throughout the depression.

The General Strike had other significant impacts on southern mills and communities, as well. Mill executives and townspeople panicked, and governors responded by imposing military control. Government officials dispatched fourteen thousand troops with machine guns and bayonets in the Carolinas. The strike was over after twenty-two days. As Zingraff (1991) reports, the activists were purged from the textile labor force, the unions lost credibility, the workers who remained on the payroll were demoralized, and the inflamed mill owners further rationalized their strategies for production and control over local communities. The fear that surrounded General Strike of 1934 was so dramatic it served to silence discussion of the historical event. Today, members of this community often deny or refuse to acknowledge the strike of 1934 (Stone and Heffner 1995).

Despite worker unrest, Cannon Mills remained a strong leader in the textile industry, as well as an influential organization in the state. Charles Cannon was a member of an elite network of state power, and his personal power extended beyond the firm and company town. It was, at least partially, responsible for the quick military response to worker insurgency. It is not surprising that the state reacted in Cannon's favor. Cannon, in cooperation with John W. Hanes, is credited with saving North Carolina from bankruptcy during the depression by obtaining credit for the state (Young 1963). Charles Cannon was extremely popular with other business owners and state officials. Both major political parties recruited him as a candidate for office in North Carolina. The Republicans had nominated him, without his knowledge, to the United States Senate in 1926, and the Democrats courted him as a possible gubernatorial candidate on several occasions. According to historians, Cannon always declined in favor of business (Young 1963). The strengths of Cannon's political ties provided a link to state power that served to benefit the firm.

In the 1940s, at Kannapolis' peak of prosperity, the mill employed more than 25,000 workers (Collins 1994). Kannapolis was the largest unincorporated town in the United States (see *Raleigh News and Observer*, September 1, 1985). Like his father, Charles Cannon opposed incorporation, probably because it would mean higher taxes for the company and loss of company control over the local labor supply. Over the next several decades, Cannon continued the paternalist style of management in both the workplace and the community. He often helped people secure loans from the local bank with a personal phone call, written note, or visit on behalf of the worker. Known as "Mr. Charlie," he was described as a "round, ruddy-faced man with an arthritic limp who wandered the cavernous mill in a work shirt, backslapping and jawing with the workers" (*Raleigh News and Observer*, September 1, 1985). As this historical overview has shown, it was the combination of traditional paternalist control and legal authority backed by state power that provided Cannon with extreme power over both the community and the workplace.

Unlike the 1920s and 1930s, the decades of the 1940s, 50s, and 60s were relatively calm for Cannon Mills. During this time, many aspects of the textile-production process remained relatively unchanged. Cannon, like many other dominant firms, benefited from the increased concentration of industry that occurred after World War II (Barkin 1982). Cannon Mills was one of the companies that grew sounder, while other, less successful textile firms collapsed. The unincorporated mill village of Kannapolis continued to be self-contained and isolated from outside industry. The tight control over the labor market provided Cannon with a stable labor supply. Charles Cannon's mill community and workplace were very insular, free from potential economic threats.

In 1961, Charles A. Cannon celebrated his 50th year with Cannon Mills. During this half century, the company created and maintained an average of a job for one additional person each day of the 18,550-day period (Ely and Larkin 1987). Cannon continued symbolic demonstrations of paternalism, such as establishing textile scholarships at state universities for employees and their children in the memory of his son, Charles A. Cannon, Jr., an Army aviator killed in World War II (Ely and Larkin 1987).

Charles Cannon protected the company's insularity by resisting outside control of his mills. In 1962, when Charles Cannon refused to solicit proxies from all of the company's common stockholders, preferring to solicit only those who held voting stock, the New York Stock Exchange Board of Commissioners removed Cannon Mills. Cannon felt the required disclosure of information was intrusive and unnecessary. At that time, the Cannon family and relatives held 40 percent of the voting stock and 27 percent of the total stock (Collins 1994). As might be expected, the removal of the company from the outside influences required by the New York Stock Exchange served to strengthen family control of the firm.

Also in 1962, the board of directors elected Don S. Holt as president and chief executive officer, with Charles Cannon becoming chairperson of the board. Cannon Mills celebrated its 75th anniversary with sales reaching $231 million (Ely and Larkin 1987). Mill expansion continued in 1964 as the company announced plans for a huge, highly automatic Scink plant (later Plant 16) that would employ 550 people. Industry experts hailed it as the largest textile mill built in the world since World War II. The new plant represented a step toward greater technological efficiency of production. Other expansions and improvements included a new towel mill in Kannapolis, an improvement in the company retirement plan, and wage advances (Ely and Larkin 1987). The upward trend continued, and 1965 was a record year in sales with $278 million. Earnings were the second best in the history of the company—$13.32 a share—and Cannon Mills won two international awards for superior marketing and packaging (Ely and Larkin 1987).

The market dominance of Cannon Mills in home furnishings continued into the 1970s. In 1971, Charles Cannon died at age 79 after suffering a heart attack at his office. At this time, Cannon Mills owned 17 plants and employed 24,000 workers, making it the largest employer in the state of North Carolina. Charles Cannon left no long-term debt and over $60 million in cash and marketable securities. Market analysts noted that 90 percent of towel and sheet consumers recognized the Cannon name (Collins 1994). Indeed, the insulated company was a powerful leader in the textile industry and in the industrialized South.

With the death of Charles Cannon, Cannon Mills stock soared on Wall Street because investors believed that new management would take advantage of the company's cash-rich, debt-free position. This was not to happen, however; Charles Cannon's handpicked successor, Don Holt, continued his mentor's policies of neither diversifying nor broadening the company's market appeal. Other mills were bringing in well-known designers to update their look, but Cannon continued to resist, relying instead on brand-name recognition. However, while company earnings had been high, growth had been very slow. In the five years before Cannon's death, sales figures had increased only two percent a year (Collins 1994).

In 1973, the board elected Harold P. Hornaday as president and chief operating officer. Even at this late date, the town of Kannapolis remained unincorporated. Cannon Mills joined with the City of Concord and Cabarrus County to construct a $37 million regional wastewater treatment plant with sufficient capacity to serve most of Cabarrus County. Cannon's participation, which facilitated completion of the public facility, reinforced and perpetuated control over the Kannapolis community.

For much of the 1970s, Cannon held onto its share of the towel market. However, serious competitors entered the market and began to challenge Cannon's top position and chip away at the company's dominant market position. In 1975, Cannon's earnings were less than those of 1965, although its sales volume had grown 42 percent since that year (Collins 1994). Nonetheless, Cannon Mills continued to expand and opened a new 840,000-square-foot sheet distribution center in 1975 (located adjacent to the towel distribution center), increasing the company's sheet distribution capacity by 75 percent (Ely and Larkin 1987).

As the company entered its 90th year in 1977, Cannon Mills had spent $20 million per year for the previous five years in plant and machinery improvements (Collins 1994). Sales for the previous year reached $453 million. In 1978, Cannon Mills acquired Wiscassett Mills Company, a major yarn producer. Sales in 1979 reached $609 million. In that year, Cannon was reinstated to the New York Stock Exchange, having given voting rights to all public shareholders and begun publishing more detailed annual reports (Collins 1994).

In 1979, following the resignation of Hornaday, Otto G. Stolz was elected president, chairperson, and CEO (Ely and Larkin 1987). According to company reports, board members asked Hornaday to leave after the firm experienced a series of decreased profits (Collins 1994). Under Stolz, Cannon Mills attempted to catch up with its competitors by updating products and entering new markets. The company diversified into the manufacturing of various items for kitchen and bath, including mats and rugs. Cannon Mills signed luxury fabric designer Robin Roberts to create a fashionable and upscale line of sheets and towels. Nonetheless, Cannon had difficulty changing its old-fashioned image, and its share of the towel market fell to below 35 percent (Collins 1994).

Cannon Mills ended the decade of the 1970s on very different terms than it started. In addition to failures within the company, the United States economy as a whole changed from prosperous and stable to a state of crisis. As Piore and Sabel note, "By the end of the 1970s, the world economy was in a state of confusion owing to the second oil-price shock, the high United States interest rates, and the worldwide recession" (1984:181). Cannon Mills, embedded in the economy, was not the only firm to experience problems; mass production corporations in general experienced these crises. However, unlike some firms that disappeared because of what Piore and Sabel (1984) refer to as the second industrial divide, Cannon Mills maintained a presence, albeit a declining one, in the United States textile-mill complex. In part, this was due to the strong base of paternalism, established almost a century prior, that enabled the firm to control the workplace and the community. For generations, mill workers in the Kannapolis area would continue to feel indebted to the Cannon family. As will be discussed shortly, this deference would prove attractive to future owners of Cannon Mills, and eventually to new industries in the area. As one interview informant noted, "what makes the area unique is the work ethic created by Charlie Cannon. Three generations of people remember him...the work ethic is strong. [These people possess] a manufacturing mentality...they're a highly productive labor force. And it's all credited to the Charlie Cannon phenomenon."

The first phase of company history, from the late 1800s to 1982, is marked by the formation of company towns, the movement of labor from farms to factories, and the one-industry domination of almost all aspects of local life. Paternalism governed both the workplace and the community. Company owners avoided worker insurgency by providing amenities in the local community (schools, recreation, housing) and the workplace (steady and stable employment). The power of the state repressed worker protests and unionization attempts. For Cannon Mills, the efficiency of vertical integration largely facilitated textile production. By starting with the raw material and producing the finished good, the Cannon family had tight control over production—what, how much, and when. Cannon benefited early on from the vertical structuring of production and did not experience a period of restructuring characteristic of other mass production firms in the 1960s and 1970s (see Piore and Sabel 1984). The relative insulation of Cannon Mills from retail market forces served to reinforce paternalistic control of workers and local communities. As I show in the next section, national and global forces would soon break down this market and spatial insulation.

PHASE II: LEVERAGED BUYOUT BY MURDOCK

In contrast to the nearly century-long domination by the Cannon family, the next phase is relatively brief, encompassing four short and extremely turbulent years. Phase II, characterized by a leveraged buyout, provides an example of an outside entrepreneur investing in a company with hopes of profit.

In 1982, David H. Murdock, a self-made millionaire from California, purchased Cannon Mills and 660 surrounding acres (including the Kannapolis business district) in a $413 million leveraged buyout (Collins 1994). During the early 1980s, mergers and acquisitions of textile companies with under-priced common stock (relative to asset value) were attractive targets for outside investors. The strategy of new owners was to reduce operating costs and improve price/earnings ratios, thereby escalating stock prices enough to yield substantial capital gains on their original investments (*Economic Intelligence Unit* 1992). For Murdock, the purpose of having a textile company was not necessarily to participate in the industry (i.e., make sheets and towels). As one community leader informant noted, Murdock did not intend to run the mills. Rather, Murdock's tactic was to invest the firm's existing capital (e.g., company pension funds) in the stock market with hopes of acquiring profits.

David Murdock's takeover of Cannon Mills caught the community by surprise. The exact reasons for the buyout are unclear, but Charles Cannon's son William was the first to sell, and the other trustees followed his example (Collins 1994). Perhaps the Cannon family grew weary of increased textile competition. It is also conceivable that the family felt free to sell the company after the death of its patriarch. Perhaps, as some interview respondents speculated, Otto Stolz, CEO and President, and possibly a few other higher-level executives, benefited financially from the deal and helped persuade members of the Cannon family. Other worker informants felt that the new owner, David Murdock, was so "slick" (i.e., a shrewd businessman) that he talked his way into a company takeover. Most likely, it was a combination of these and other factors, embedded in a period of United States economic mergers and takeovers, which promoted family disinvestments.

Regardless of the reason, after a $413 million leveraged buyout, Murdock took the company private (Collins 1994). Murdock became chairperson and CEO, replacing Stolz, who resigned. Murdock aggressively set out to alter the way Cannon did business, a goal that would affect paternalism, production efficiency, and worker control. He announced plans for a $200 million capital improvement program, primarily for new machinery and technology (Ely and Larkin 1987). Murdock, hoping to recapture the towel and sheet market, sought to increase sales by updating the company with a glamorous and trendy image.

In 1983, the board of directors elected then vice-chairperson Harold M. Messier, Jr., president and chief operating officer; Murdock continued as the company's chair. Cannon Royal Touch, a new type of "soft touch" towel, created a market sensation. The next year, Cannon Mills won the North Carolina Governor's New Product Award (Ely and Larkin 1987). It is plausible to view the recognition as a symbol of the company's continued influence at the state level and the re-affirmed ties with new (non-local) management.

During this time, workers and community members experienced a confusing mix of paternalistic gestures and corporate greed. For example, Murdock instigated new employee health benefits and allowed workers to own the mill houses where they lived (Ely and Larkin 1987). He donated land, cash, and company labor to help Kannapolis build a senior citizen's center, park, and library (Collins 1994). In doing so, Murdock reinforced the traditional mechanisms of worker and locality control.

Nevertheless, other changes initiated by Murdock brought disruption for workers and deviated from traditional forms of paternalism. The "opportunity" to buy mill housing resulted in problems—one of which was the undermining of mill-village uniformity. The following excerpt from an interview describes the feelings of Emma, a middle-aged black woman whose mother worked in the mills during the 1980s:

> When David Murdock bought it [Cannon Mills]...individuals who lived in the mill homes had an option to buy their homes and no longer rent from Cannon Mills, but become a home owner. And have you walked through the village? Do you see the different houses that have been moved to different places...and you'll see the different colors...those are people who bought their homes. Before, all the houses were white and uniform. Based on the street and the size, everything was basically the same. And individuals who had the opportunity to purchase their home usually did something a little differently. They painted it a pastel color, put up new shutters, and just did real ownership, home ownership. And made them look different from the other homes, because they had...autonomy to do that. It was theirs now. So my mom painted her house this ugly yellow, and she went from [renting] to be a home owner. Which there was no other way that she could have owned a home based on her salary when she used to be a weaver....

As Emma suggests, Murdock's decision to sell company housing provided opportunities for autonomy and home ownership to some—a shift away from traditional paternalistic obligation—but also began the process of transforming the mill community's solidarity.

Secondly, not all workers were able to participate in the opportunity for home ownership. Although the average price for mill houses was $20,000 (*Raleigh News and Observer*, September 1, 1985), this amount was still beyond the means of many workers. As one interview informant noted, workers living in company houses "hadn't saved a dime...and I can't blame them a bit." The strong tradition of paternalism, which had provided workers with community resources, resulted in financial dependency. Typical workers, assuming the company would at least minimally meet their needs, had no reason or incentive to save the little extra money they earned. In addition, many of the workers who purchased their homes with bank loans faced serious financial problems when their jobs were cut as part of Murdock's later company restructuring.

At the same time mill workers were struggling to adjust to changes in home ownership, Murdock was making other changes that would hasten the demise of the isolated mill village. He rebuilt Charles Cannon's austere colonial home, "For Pity's Sake," and replaced it with a sprawling $1.5 million home and conference center resembling a Swiss chalet (*Raleigh News and Observer*, September 1, 1985). Murdock traveled between his California home and Kannapolis in a private jet, quickly acquiring the reputation of an "absentee landlord" by appearing primarily for groundbreakings, ribbon-cuttings, and anti-union campaign speeches. In doing so, Murdock cut the spatial connections between owner and mill workers.

Murdock's redevelopment of downtown Kannapolis also affected the insularity of the mill village culture. Murdock had four blocks in the town's center remodeled and leased as factory outlet stores in hopes of drawing tourists from nearby I-85. The redesigned Cannon Village opened for business in the fall of 1984. In its first year, there were 20 stores anchored by a large Cannon outlet. The redevelopments made many of the established merchants bitter when they had to pay higher rent or move to make room for the theme mall (*Raleigh News and Observer*, September 1, 1985).

Murdock also implemented changes in production and marketing with the goal of increasing efficiency. Notwithstanding the success of the company under family ownership, company reports note that under family management, Cannon Mills suffered from a variety of problems, including weak marketing and product designs, few financial controls, the absence of a management information system to track costs, inefficient job assignments, and overstaffing. Analysts credit much of the so-called "inefficiency" to Cannon's paternalistic interest in maintaining jobs during slack periods and his failure to acknowledge changing market demands (Collins 1994). With teams of industrial engineers to evaluate plant efficiency and revise jobs and salaries, Murdock created significant changes in the work-place.

Murdock reorganized the design department, doubling it in size, releasing its manager, and discontinuing most of the existing towel and sheet designs. As Collins reports (1994), Murdock hired Japanese designer Issey Miyake and Swedish designer Katja to create lines for Cannon Mills. The company launched a racy advertising campaign featuring various celebrities between Cannon sheets with the statement, "Two of the most famous names in America sleep together." Cannon Mills marketed towels at all price levels, including a line that competed directly with archrival Fieldcrest's Royal Velvet. Murdock and his staff also enlisted mass merchandising in an effort to increase profits. For example, the producers of the nighttime soap opera Dynasty signed an agreement that allowed Cannon Mills to produce a Dynasty collection, patterned after the sets used on the show (Collins 1994).

Despite Murdock's attempts to invigorate the company, Cannon Mills continued to lose money. Murdock's short-term business mentality, with an emphasis on quick profits, meant that Cannon was not preparing for the future. In addition, for the first time, domestic textile firms faced competition from imports. Murdock responded to globalization with the ultimate form of worker control—further layoffs (3,000 between 1982 and 1986) and the closing of three mills (Collins 1994). In general, Murdock tended to be reactive to market trends and global processes rather than being at the forefront of change. The short-term/quick profit strategy would turn out to be a long-term problem for Cannon Mills.

Murdock's steps are consistent with general industry trends in the 1980s that included significant investments in equipment and new technology, downsizing in the form of employment reduction, and "niche" marketing; these changes represent steps toward increased production efficiency. Though perhaps consistent with business principles of the day, Murdock's strategies did not appeal to workers in Cannon Mills.

In reaction to the massive changes within the firm, including steps to increase production and worker control, the Amalgamated Clothing and Textile Workers Union (ACTWU) attempted to organize Cannon employees. The union had failed previously, most recently in 1974 by a 44 to 56 percent vote, but brought the issue to election in October of 1985. Murdock, by that time already seeking a buyer for Cannon, fought the union in a bitter campaign, jetting frequently into Kannapolis, touring the factories, and shaking hands with company employees (Ely and Larkin 1987). Interview data support this, as multiple respondents attested to a strong display of anti-union tactics. One woman claimed Murdock appeared on television crying, and that the company placed full-page newspaper advertisements discouraging workers from supporting the union. Local social institutions, including merchants, churches, and the media, reinforced the purported negative consequences of the union. Local merchants threatened to revoke credit for union supporters. As is common under these conditions (Billings 1990), the movement to unionize was defeated in a 27 to 63 percent vote (Collins 1994; Ely and Larkin 1987).

The union drive represented an attempt by workers to establish equal social relations between themselves and owners. Workers wanted better working conditions and secure employment. Nevertheless, the struggle was embedded in a paternalistic local community, where various social institutions continued to reinforce company policy. As the overwhelming defeat suggests, many workers remained committed to the company. Even so, the brief period of Murdock's ownership changed the social relationships among community members and the company. Members of the mill community, many of whom had lost their jobs, were becoming increasingly critical of the company. Workers who continued in the plants became less willing to tolerate unfair practices. As the unionization drive demonstrated, these people had the ability to organize and resist oppression. Although unsuccessful in terms of achieving union certification, the insurgency brought attention and raised awareness, strengthening worker solidarity. As Murdock dismantled the structural basis of paternalism for the sake of production efficiency, the firm's control of workers was becoming unsure and less stable. The union involvement was a challenge to the community's social isolation.

Within a few months, the second most significant turnover in Cannon Mills' history occurred. In January 1986, Murdock sold approximately 75 percent of Cannon Mills to Fieldcrest Mills for $321 million (Collins 1994). The sale did not dissolve Murdock's relationship with the firm and community, however. He retained real estate holdings, which included most of the commercial real estate in downtown Kannapolis, worth approximately $100 million.

In addition, Murdock absconded with around $25 million from the Cannon pension fund that he had ended shortly before the completion of the sale. In October 1986, the ACTWU filed suit, charging that Murdock had mishandled the funds and thus violated his fiduciary duties as a trustee of the plan. As reported by Collins (1994), the point of contention was Murdock's use of pension funds while he was trying to gain control of Occidental Petroleum. Murdock had started acquiring Occidental stock in 1981. In February 1982, Occidental elected Murdock as director under conditions that barred him from acquiring more than five percent of its stock. Late in that year, the Cannon pension fund began to purchase Occidental stock, which by 1984 accounted for 7.8 percent of the fund's holdings. In 1984, Occidental repurchased its stock from Murdock-controlled entities, including the Cannon pension fund, with a $60 million premium attached. After Murdock terminated the pension fund in 1985, the fund's excess assets, including the profits from the Occidental deal, were folded back into Murdock's other entities. The union's suit charged that Murdock had used the funds to either "greenmail" or to take over Occidental, as opposed to managing the funds for its participants and beneficiaries, and that he had used the funds similarly in actions against Kaiser Cement. ACTWU and Cannon Mills settled the case out of court in 1989 for a reported $1 million, leaving Murdock with $59 million.

Upon the liquidation of the pension plan, Murdock invested the remaining funds with Executive Life Insurance of California. The company, which had invested heavily in junk bonds underwritten by Michael Milken of Drexel Burnham Lambert during the 1980s, suffered sharp losses after the junk bond industry collapsed in 1990. In April 1991, state regulators seized the assets of Executive Life Insurance; Cannon cut monthly pension payments by 30 percent (Collins 1994). Once again, this situation was common for the time. During takeovers, company owners often depleted pension funds from the employees' plans and substituted inferior plans of less value (Zey 1993). The era of junk bond investing was led by extreme individual greed, all too often at the expense of the company and its employees.

During this phase of company history, from 1982-1986, mergers, takeovers, and changes in production constituted restructuring within the United States textile-mill complex. Murdock's purchase of Cannon is one example. The simultaneous closing of outdated plants and the sale of mill housing facilitated new forms of community organization. Murdock was on a "smokestack chase," characterized by a quick-profit mentality (Grant and Hutchinson 1996). The drive for increased revenue led to changes in community and firm relations, including the demise of many paternalistic gestures. Most significantly, Murdock robbed lifetime workers in Cannon Mills of retirement benefits.

Ironically, paternalism, based on personal and family imagery, was able to transcend the end of family rule. This deeply rooted structure enabled Murdock to ride the coattails of the "Charlie Cannon phenomenon" without investing much of his own time and money. Why? Perhaps it was a reflection of the continuing monopoly in the local labor market, or the result of increased job insecurity in the 1980s, or a combination of these and other effects.

It is important to note that during Murdock's reign, the marketing efforts of Cannon Mills remained focused on the national retail market. As a result, the company's responses to globalization were inadequate and the once insulated firm was floundering on a market that was now international. As will be shown in the next section, Murdock's reaction was simple and predictable—it was time to sell the company. The next section brings the history of the firm to the modern era, from 1986 to the present.

PHASE III: ACQUISITION OF CANNON BY FIELDCREST MILLS

The third phase in the history of the firm provides an example of corporate merger, a frequent occurrence in the 1980s (Harrison and Bluestone 1988). Murdock sold Cannon Mills because he was losing money and getting into legal trouble. For Fieldcrest, already a leader in the United States textile industry, the goal of the merger was to increase concentration and market dominance. As will be presented, the merged company of Fieldcrest Cannon relied even less on paternalism as a form of control. Instead, the firm was able to rely on strong anti-union tactics and a new labor supply made up of immigrant workers. The labor context of this time was one of corporate streamlining and downsizing, reducing employment and wages (Harrison and Bluestone 1988).

In January of 1986, Fieldcrest paid $321 million to David Murdock for the Cannon Mills name and its sheet, towel, and rug plants. The amount was substantially less than the $413 million Murdock paid in 1982 (Collins 1994). Historical accounts speculate that Murdock wanted out of a losing business. Informant interviews and news accounts suggest that Murdock was "a shrewd businessman...only out for his own financial benefit." Regardless of his motives, the acquisition of Cannon by Fieldcrest propelled the company to the number one position in the towel market, number one in the blanket market, and number three in the sheet market.

Later that year, Fieldcrest Cannon purchased Bigelow-Sanford, Inc., a South Carolina manufacturer of residential and industrial contract carpeting. A group of executives had purchased Bigelow-Sanford in 1981, and in turn sold it to Fieldcrest in December 1986 for $129 million—$4 million in cash and 460,727 shares of Fieldcrest common stock. After the acquisition, Fieldcrest merged Bigelow-Sanford with its Karastan division and dismissed the Bigelow-Sanford executives. Soon thereafter, rival carpetmaker DuPont introduced its Stainmaster fiber, which was enormously popular but proved to be very difficult to dye into the carpet colors that consumers wanted. Fieldcrest, heavily in debt from acquisitions and lacking a knowledgeable staff in carpet operations, committed large capital outlays in an attempt to master the process and secure this market niche (Collins 1994).

However, attempts to dominate the carpet market were unsuccessful. In 1987, Fieldcrest lost $3.7 million; much of the loss was attributed to problems with Biglow-Sanford. Fieldcrest restructured in 1988, creating three divisions (Fieldcrest, Cannon, and Karastan Bigelow) with separate corporate management and sales forces but with shared manufacturing facilities to lower production costs (Collins 1994). While the use of common production facilities increased production efficiency, it resulted in a decline in the overall number of jobs in local textile communities.

Fieldcrest announced that it wanted out of the carpet business altogether and was looking for a buyer. The re-prioritizing of capital commitments helped temporarily to boost profits to $11.3 million that year, reaching

$23.4 million in 1989. In 1990, however, the company posted a $38 million loss on $1.24 billion in sales. The company's stock value, which had peaked in 1986 at $43, dropped to below six dollars per share (Collins 1994).

The drop led Fieldcrest to begin a series of cost-cutting measures under its new chairperson, James Fitzgibbons. Fitzgibbons reduced the workforce by 1,700, discontinued an unprofitable automatic blanket operation, and unloaded inventory. In addition to cuts in the number of jobs, the reduction in inventory meant that production became sporadic instead of constant, with the company laying off workers and calling them in on an as-needed basis.

Provoked by job cuts and alleged unfair labor practices, workers in the Kannapolis plants attempted to unionize in 1991. As one interview informant stated, "People had gone 3-4 years without a raise, conditions were bad." In response, the firm instigated an all out anti-union campaign that included local merchants, churches, and lawyers. The company paid to bring two groups of lawyers to town, one for white workers and one for black workers, to convince employees that the union was not in their best interest. In primary interview data, several respondents claimed that local ministers who spoke out against the union during this period received gifts, such as church organs and vans. The firm used racist threats to fracture union support such as telling whites they would have black supervisors if the union was to be instated (informant interview). Nonetheless, the vote was close. The union lost by only 199 votes out of more than 6,000 ballots cast in the election (*Raleigh News and Observer*, September 6, 1995). Several respondents claimed that the company used unfair tactics to defeat the union, such as registering and voting in the names of deceased people, posting threats of deportation in Spanish, and drawing artificial lines to keep union organizers away from the plant.

The workers' claims proved valid. In 1995, after four years of litigation, the National Labor Relations Board (NLRB) charged Fieldcrest Cannon with unfair labor practices. Among other things, the NLRB found the company guilty of intimidation, coercion, and harassment of employees. On September 4, 1995, the NLRB affirmed a decision of an administrative law judge and demanded that Fieldcrest Cannon award $2 million in back pay to employees who were denied a wage increase on the basis of their support for the union. Additionally, the NLRB demanded the reinstatement of 13 union supporters fired by the company during the 1991 election in Kannapolis. The workers were also to receive back pay of up to $500,000 (*Martinsville Bulletin*, September 5, 1995; *Raleigh News and Observer*, September 6, 1995).

The NLRB deemed the unfair labor practices by the company so numerous and pervasive that it required Fieldcrest Cannon's vice president for human resources, Ozzie Raines, to personally read or be present for the announcement of a 45-point cease-and-desist notice in English and Spanish. The NLRB ordered the company to publish the notice in local papers twice a week for four weeks and mail copies of the notice to all employees. In its decision, the NLRB ruled that Fieldcrest Cannon had lost the right to hold the next union election on its own premises because of objectionable conduct in the past (*Martinsville Bulletin*, September 5, 1995; *Raleigh News and Observer*, September 6, 1995).

However, worker control and unionization struggles were only part of the obstacles faced by Fieldcrest Cannon in the early 1990s. Unable to find a buyer for its rug and carpet division (Bigelow-Sanford), the company had consolidated those operations, hoping to increase profits. In mid-1992, the company refinanced its loan agreements, reducing its interest payments. Nevertheless, Fieldcrest had experienced lower sales from 1988 to 1992, largely because of a $136 million decline in carpet and rug sales (Collins 1994). Fieldcrest Cannon continued restructuring, shifting production by closing a towel plant in York, South Carolina, establishing a separate blanket division, and entering a venture with the Institute of Textile Technology to increase production efficiency (*Hoover's Handbook Database* 1996).

Fieldcrest Cannon spent most of 1993 fending off a buyout offer from one of its major competitors, Springs Industries. Springs tried to buy Fieldcrest's stock and the stock of Amoskeag Company, a firm that controlled about 80% of Fieldcrest's voting stock and 30% of its equity. The matter was resolved when Fieldcrest purchased Amoskeag later that year for $138 million (Hoover 1996). The capital for this purchase came from the sale of Bigelow-Sanford to Mohawk Industries for $148 million in July 1993. That ended Fieldcrest Cannon's futile attempts to profit from carpet production.

The passage of NAFTA in 1993 enabled Fieldcrest Cannon to open a showroom and warehouse in Mexico. The company continued to expand its global presence by setting up a distributor in Brazil for its bed, bath, and blanket products and obtaining the manufacturing and distribution business and trademark for Canada's leading towel brand, Caldwell (Hoover 1996). Also in 1993, Fieldcrest Cannon secured the profitable license to manufacture home textile products for the 1996 Olympic Games, held in Atlanta, Georgia. To support these new ventures, the firm built a state-of-the-art weaving plant in Alabama. The new facility incorporates innovative technology, including computer-aided machinery, making it one of the most modern towel-weaving facilities in the world (Hoover 1996).

In 1994, the company branched into the bath fashions market with the launch of a collection of shower curtains and bath ceramics, and it expanded the line of licensed Olympic products. Fieldcrest Cannon acquired the Sure Fit furniture-covering business of UTC Holdings (with 75% of the furniture covering market and $55 million in sales) in 1995 (Hoover 1996).

The firm's restructuring of the 1990s is in part a response to globalization. The "niches" sought by the firm, however, tended to rely on national markets. Nonetheless, because the firm is embedded in a changing economy, global trends necessitated responses via restructuring. The alternative was to risk losing market dominance. Unlike the era of Cannon, when one production strategy was sufficient for a century, the less stable modern economy requires constant adjustments.

In 1995, Fieldcrest Cannon reorganized its New York operations, resulting in the relocation of 20 percent of its 124 New York employees to Kannapolis, North Carolina (*Martinsville Bulletin*, February 28, 1995). Employees moved included the company's division presidents, and marketing and operations personnel. The remaining New York employees either took early retirement or were dismissed. Fieldcrest Cannon Plant #1, in Kannapolis, which had previously employed 6,800 workers, now houses a new 42,000-square-foot computer data center. The company relocated and consolidated all of its mainframe computers in the center. The company brought 140 information-technology professionals to Kannapolis to work in the data center (*Wall Street Journal*, August 12, 1996). CEO Fitzgibbons claimed the new data center is a key element of Fieldcrest Cannon's information services strategy, essential to "customer-oriented, world class manufacturing and service" (*Fieldcrest Cannon Today*, October 1994). More recently, Fieldcrest Cannon contracted with Lockheed Martin Corporation to provide information and technology services.

The centralization of information processing will improve the integration of production and marketing. Fieldcrest Cannon will be better able to respond to consumer demands through computerized strategies such as just-in-time and quick response. As the effects of restructuring trickle down, opportunities for traditional, established employees decrease. The most obvious example is the replacement of workers with computers at both the shop floor and information-processing levels. Not only are jobs cut and redefined, but relations among remaining workers and management are also transformed. As Zuboff (1988) reminds us, computer-based technologies are not neutral. Rather, all technologies embody essential characteristics that will alter the nature of work. As will be presented in Chapter Six, technology has consequences for worker control.

Other examples of Fieldcrest Cannon's efforts to centralize and concentrate production exist. In March 1996, the company closed two manufacturing plants as part of a continuing campaign to cut costs. According to a *Wall Street Journal* report, Fieldcrest Cannon claimed it would eventually save $8 million to $9 million in annual operating expenses by closing a towel manufacturing facility in York, South Carolina and a yarn plant in Concord, North Carolina. The two facilities employed over 500 workers. According to one interview informant, a mill worker, these plants contained old equipment that the company had failed to update. James M.

Fitzgibbons, chair and chief executive officer, made the following statement:

> We are committed to modernizing the systems, processes, and facilities that will position Fieldcrest Cannon to better service our customers and achieve consistent financial performance over the long run. To do this, we must aggressively remove costs from our systems, streamline our processes and utilize all assets more effectively. Reducing the size of our work force is a difficult but necessary part of this process. Our employees in Concord and York have worked diligently for this company. We will make every attempt to assist them in securing employment opportunities. Furthermore, these closing are not related to NAFTA or the effect of foreign imports on our textile industry. We are not transferring any production from these facilities to offshore plants (*Southern Textile News*, March 18, 1996; *Wall Street Journal* On-Line, March 4, 1996).

Echoes of paternalism remain in comments such as these. However, more important is the emphasis on effective performance and accumulation as achieved through consolidation. Fitzgibbons, chair and CEO of Fieldcrest in the 1990s, served as the president of the American Textile Manufacturers Institute (ATMI). In an interview with *Textile World* (March 1996 p. 35), he states his belief that the industry-wide consolidation will continue:

> I think it's inevitable. If you look at the distribution of our products, there are fewer stores and fewer chains handling bigger and bigger chunks of business. Wal-Mart is going to top $100 billion this year. Sears has been the most successful retailer in any category of soft apparel. The little guys are dropping out. I think it's going to take size and systems to satisfy huge retailers.

Fitzgibbons' statement exemplifies a strategy that began at the end of the first phase of the company—to be one of the top textile firms, it is necessary to consolidate and streamline by updating the production process and eliminating outdated equipment and surplus workers. This type of firm-level restructuring results in decreased numbers of production jobs. Plants close and relocate key machinery and people to a new centralized location. Firms such as Fieldcrest Cannon no longer control retail outlets. Concentration in retailing has forced firms to increase efficiency to meet the demands of national chains. With the opening of local labor markets to new industries, single firms are less likely to control communities that surround textile mills, such as Kannapolis. Company domination of the locality slowly dissipates. As will be discussed in the next chapter, workers often have increased employment options.

As with most mergers, the consolidation of firms decreased the number of jobs. In an effort to centralize and concentrate production, Fieldcrest Cannon sold inefficient divisions (including electric blanket and carpet production facilities). The firm opened new plants and expanded production in other areas, such as rural areas of Georgia and Alabama. Finally, the company introduced a large amount of automated machinery. All resulted in job losses for many employees.

Increased competition, stemming from the globalization of the economy, necessitated firm restructuring. In contrast to Murdock's ownership (where the key concern was immediate profits regardless of industry status), the goal of Fieldcrest Cannon has been to dominate the retail market and ensure a semi-monopolistic standing. Indeed, by merging with and over-taking its most serious competitor (Cannon Mills), Fieldcrest enhanced its position of dominance and market control. The modern firm also provides a contrast to the paternalism of early Cannon ownership that continued into Murdock's reign. The new firm provided little community support, brought in new workers to replace existing ones, closed many local plants, and began the outsourcing of production.

Control over the locality decreases as the firm shifts from local to regional labor markets. The company no longer relies on paternalism as a means of worker control. Instead, the firm utilizes restructured market relations to control workers. New equipment continues to replace workers. Outdated plants are closed. New forms of spatialization emerge as new production facilities are located in low-wage, non-insurgent areas and the company outsources some aspects of production. Partly a response to increased global competition and dominance of retail markets, recent changes at Fieldcrest Cannon have decreased the number of textile jobs and broken down the base of paternalism. In many ways, the community's social isolation, or the traditional mill village, no longer exists.

CONCLUSION

Globalization, restructuring, and spatialization are dominant forces that have shaped the history and have an effect on the status of Fieldcrest Cannon. However, the effects to the company occur in different degrees. For example, while the firm is influenced by the existence of a global market, the size of the domestic market (in which Fieldcrest Cannon is a leading supplier of towels and sheets) has not made it necessary for the firm to seek overseas markets. Thus, Fieldcrest Cannon has had little involvement with exporting and importing. A quote from a company executive illustrates this:

> Because domestic textiles have a lot of bulk, they don't usually get shipped overseas...it's not cheap freight. So, the companies will build plants in other markets which they serve. Years ago, we had

a plant in Ireland. It failed because the company tried to force their technology and product on the European market. Our company has done business with Mexico, but it wasn't easy. Currency fluctuations are a problem...regulations to get goods into Mexico are complicated...their way of doing business is not ours...with other countries, you've got to think like they do, follow their customs.

The lack of international involvement does not suggest that the firm is unaffected by globalization. Because Fieldcrest Cannon is embedded in an economy that *does* operate within a global market, the company *is* affected by globalization. However, the responses taken by the firm indicate a conscious decision to emphasize its national market. The home furnishing sector of the textile-mill complex is much more insulated from global competition than the apparel sector. Unlike apparel production, which requires a greater number of workers, the production of towels and sheets can be highly automated, and companies can find adequate cheap labor in the United States. Sheet and towel production is relatively simple; most sewing and cutting is on a straight line. Production typically uses few embellishments, meaning almost no outsourcing of production (see Chapter Three). In other words, firms save little, if any, money by sending products elsewhere to be finished. Thus, companies like Fieldcrest Cannon do not search for international production sites. Likewise, the drive to reach international markets is limited because United States firms typically receive adequate demand from the national market.

The restructuring process, however, has directly affected Fieldcrest Cannon as the textile industry moves toward more flexible, consumer-driven production. The economic restructuring of the 1980s and 1990s, driven by the goal of capital accumulation, includes technological developments enabling production that is more efficient. A re-organization of work and labor process accompanied the three phases of company history: automation (shuttleless looms, programmable machines), employee dismissals, plant closings, and a fundamental alteration of community relations, including the sale of company housing, decreased mill employment, and the replacement of paternalism with bureaucratic authority relations. Largely, changes started with the death of Charles Cannon in 1971. Before this, Cannon Mills had been riding on market dominance left over from World War II years. Charles Cannon and his successor refused to diversify. Cannon invested in upgrades, but it was too late. Murdock took over, and with massive upgrades the new owner implemented a consumer-driven production process.

The firm is in a period of transition. It is modernizing and automating. The power of the firm is contingent and embedded. Will it ever develop a fully automated mill? Probably not, according to industry leaders, who suggest that firms will not develop automated mills as "add-ons." Rather, they will be new entities built from the ground up. Fieldcrest Cannon has added some automated plants and central processing centers. Concentration in retailing has forced firms to cut production costs to maintain contracts with the large national chains (e.g., Wal-Mart). In response, firms like Fieldcrest Cannon are attempting to use computer modeling and forecasting to link their production facilities with retailers in order to further rationalize production and marketing.

We can understand the unevenness of change and variation by examining the process of spatialization that is evident in each historical phase. James Cannon choose to buy land near existing plants and capture local labor markets. Charles Cannon followed this pattern by not allowing incorporation of Kannapolis. After the Cannon family rule, however, other industries moved into the area. This did not bother new owner David Murdock, as he was busy cutting jobs (with automation) and needed fewer and fewer workers. During this time, the mill village began disintegrating. By the time Cannon Mills merged with Fieldcrest, the old patterns of spatial control were dissolved. The firm closed plants and cut jobs; new industries entered the labor market to capture the surplus supply of cheap labor. This trend escalated in the 1990s as Fieldcrest Cannon expanded to new regions with different labor market structures.

The evidence presented in the three phases of company history illustrates the changing significance of paternalism and structural-exploitation. Beginning with Cannon, the company instilled strong mechanisms of formal and informal control in both the community and workplace. These systems transcended the end of family rule and continued to exist during Murdock's ownership of the mills. However, in the current period of ownership, the company does not rely on the paternalistic deference of workers. Rather, the restructured flexibility of production, in the active context of a global economy, has created an environment that enables owners to control workers through an expanded labor pool, outsourcing, and technological advances that decrease the need for workers.

In addition, it is clear that increased production efficiency, often associated with technological advancements, is a means for the company to increase profits and market dominance. From the early days of vertical integration to the current possibility of a "lights out," fully automatic plant, company owners have sought means of enhancing the process of capital accumulation.

As the history of the firm demonstrates, the firm is embedded in a local community, in the textile-mill complex, and in the world textile industry. The processes of globalization, restructuring, and spatialization influence social relationships among community, firm, and market. Not only does the firm mirror changes in the United States textile-mill complex, but it also reflects changes in the market economy (e.g., mergers and downsizing). Nevertheless, analysis of processes at this level does little to explain social impacts on community members and workers. What is life like for people who live in the ex-mill village of Kannapolis? How do the processes of social change impact the remaining mill workers? These and related questions are addressed in Chapters Six and Seven.

Chapter Six

Community Outcomes
Remaking Social Relationships

The purpose of this chapter is twofold. First, I demonstrate the significance of the effects of globalization, restructuring, and spatialization on a particular labor market area. Included in this discussion will be evidence of change in Cabarrus County and Kannapolis, North Carolina. Second, I address the question: what are the social impacts of the processes for the community of Kannapolis? Interpretation centers on the topics of race and household survival strategies.

A key theoretical assumption that underlies this chapter is that processes of change, including globalization, restructuring, and spatialization, are embedded in local contexts (see also McMichael 1996). The impacts of the processes, however, are uneven and vary across time and place. One way to capture the varying dimensions of inequality is to focus on *social location* or the position of an area in time and place, and to link uneven changes across different spatial analytical levels (Lobao 1996). By using the larger social structure to focus on localities, power relations, and culture, we expose the embeddedness of processes (see also Lobao 1996; Mingione 1991). Because places are nested within others at different spatial scales, processes at one spatial scale influence those at another. This is particularly important for our understanding of how global processes create changes at national and local levels.

Previous literature suggests that communities that have undergone some form of economic restructuring resulting from globalization and spatialization experience certain repercussions (Bluestone and Harrison 1982, Harrison and Bluestone 1988). In a study of communities in rural Ontario, Leach and Winson (1995) found that the long-term effects of restructuring are negative for workers and their communities. For most respondents in this study, restructuring brought about a substantial drop in household income, even when reemployment occurred. Additionally, the quality of work deteriorated for most upon reemployment. Respondents reported extra stress in securing new jobs, worse job conditions, and increased commuting distances. The work of Fitchen (1991, 1995) supports the claim that restructuring negatively affects communities, especially where the town has lost a major employer. Impacts include dramatic increases in poverty rates, welfare rolls, and service needs. Finally, as Johnson (1990) points out, the process of economic restructuring may alter forms of inequality. Drawing on a case study of the Australian textile industry, she argued that the reconstitution of patriarchy (in terms of a new patriarchal economy and restatement of male power) did not happen by chance, but was part of industrial restructuring to increase profits.

As these studies suggest, restructuring affects communities, primarily in negative ways. What about Kannapolis? How have the social processes of change, including globalization, restructuring, and spatialization, impacted this textile-mill community? In this chapter, I focus on the period between 1980 and 1990, one in which changes in firm ownership occurred and, consequently, an era when long-standing patterns of paternalism, technological efficiency, and worker control were most dramatically altered. Additionally, for textiles, this was a decade of industry-wide mergers (see Chapter Four) and increased international market expansion (see Chapter Three). By comparing 1980 and 1990 census data, we are able to document the changes that occurred in labor market patterns.

LABOR MARKET CHANGES

For this case, the labor market is defined as three nested geographical areas: 1) the immediate community surrounding the mills, the town of Kannapolis, North Carolina; 2) the county surrounding Kannapolis, Cabarrus County, North Carolina; and 3) the labor market area defined by 1990 Census data (LMA 009) that encompasses Kannapolis, Cabarrus County, and other counties in the area. Qualitative and quantitative data provide evidence of change in Kannapolis, Cabarrus County, and the surrounding labor market area. Combined with analysis from industry and firm levels, these data contribute to the understanding of the social impacts of change in the textile industry.

What does the concept labor market mean? The term *labor market* is used to describe a locality or community defined by a set of relations between buyers and sellers of labor. Local labor markets consist of opportunity structures formed in part by national and regional macroeconomic forces and by the local social and economic organization of production (Killian and Tolbert 1993). Labor markets provide a useful context in which to examine the work patterns of community members and extend our understanding of change by not limiting the affected areas to any specific city or township. For example, the labor force in rural areas of the United States has long been dependent upon the manufacturing sector as a primary employer. These areas historically attracted manufacturing firms because they offered a pool of relatively low-skilled, low-waged labor suitable for production lines (Killian and Porterfield 1994). By examining broad-based areas as labor markets, researchers have been able to gain an understanding of the buying and selling of labor that is not limited by city or county boundaries.

The concept of labor market is extremely relevant to the study of the textile industry insofar as firms have had a tendency to locate in areas void of other industry, providing a captive labor supply and enabling the textile firm to dominate the locality (e.g., company towns). Labor markets provide an excellent illustration of the process of spatialization, or the idea that domination and subordination within an industry may vary across time and place. An employer's use (or threat) of spatial relocation of production facilities serves as a key labor-control strategy.

As described in Chapter One, a significant amount of textile production in the United States occurs in the South, especially North Carolina, South Carolina, and Georgia, where labor has traditionally been low-paid and non-unionized. It is within this area that the present case is located. Kannapolis, North Carolina is the site of Fieldcrest Cannon Mills (now a subsidiary of Pillowtex, Inc.). With a city population in 1990 of 29,696, Kannapolis is located in the Piedmont region of North Carolina. Historically, this area was rich in cotton. Accounts report that in 1878, the area operated at least three cotton gins, indicating a consistent cotton crop (Moore and Wingate 1940).

The *labor market area* (LMA) surrounding Kannapolis provides a useful definition of locality. A fundamental premise behind the use of LMAs is that county boundaries are not adequate in defining the economy of an area. County lines do not confine local economies; they are more accurately conceptualized as the interrelationships between buyers and sellers of labor (Tolbert and Killian 1987). This is true in the case of textile manufacturing, where mills, housing, workers, and company owners are often spread across several counties.

Researchers use commuting-to-work patterns, based on Census data, to operationalize labor market areas (LMAs). In the 1980s, a group of rural sociologists and agricultural economists began a research project to identify and measure the characteristics of local labor markets as basic units of social and economic organization (see Tolbert and Killian 1987). Researchers developed LMAs for 1980 and 1990 using United States Census journey-to-work information for counties and county equivalents in the 50 states and the District of Columbia. Once defined, however, LMA boundaries may change, and these changes reflect transformations in the organization of work and commuting patterns (see Singlemann and Deseran, 1993, for examples of research utilizing LMAs).

The labor market area in this extended case study for 1990 is identified as LMA 009 and consists of the following counties: Union, Mecklenburg,

Anson, Cabarrus, Chester, Stanly, Rowan (North Carolina) and York and
Lancaster (South Carolina), and reflects a change from the 1980 LMA. In
1980, the area was represented by two LMAs, one that included Anson,
Cabarrus, Rowan counties (LMA 338) and another containing
Mecklenburg, Lincoln, Union, Stanly, York, Lancaster, and Chester (LMA
339). LMAs 338 and 339, minus Lincoln County, combined to form the
1990 LMA that includes Kannapolis and Cabarrus County.

The fact that Charlotte-Mecklenburg County and Kannapolis-Cabarrus
County were in separate LMAs in 1980 is significant. The areas had separate patterns of work and commuting. The change in commuting-to-work
patterns between the 1980 and 1990 Census is an indication of change in
local labor markets, or the pattern of buying and selling labor. The number
of commuters leaving Cabarrus County and traveling to work in
Mecklenburg County doubled from 1980 (8,463) to 1990 (16,603) (United
States Census 1990). The alteration of the LMA is a consequence of the
process of spatialization and directly relates to the decline of textile dominance, changing patterns of employment, and the emergence of new urban
centers.

Charlotte, North Carolina, located in Mecklenburg County, has a history as a business center for the industrial counties of the southern Piedmont
and has become a nationally prominent financial and retail distribution
center. New factories that were unrelated to textiles came to Mecklenburg
County and made it one of the state's top industrial counties (Stuart 1993).
Charlotte is a major airport hub, and its international flights helped draw
foreign firms to the area. In 1992, 260 foreign firms had their United States
headquarters in North Carolina, and over half (138 firms) were located
within the 1990 LMA 009, the majority (120) being in Mecklenburg
County (Stuart 1993). Combined 1990 United States Census estimates for
each of the nine counties in the LMA indicate a population of approximately 1.1 million people. Mecklenburg County alone contains just under
half of the LMA population (46 percent), and while most workers in each
of the nine counties were employed in either technical or machinery occupations, Mecklenburg County had the highest concentration of managers
and technicians. Farm workers made up a very small percentage of all
workers in the nine-county area (United States Census 1990).

Mecklenburg County's population, while large, is not sufficient to meet
the labor needs of its growing economy, an imbalance that has resulted in
a dramatic rise in inter-county commuting and has changed the relationships between Charlotte-Mecklenburg and the counties that surround it
(Stuart 1993). Each county no longer exists as an autonomous economic
unit; rather, they are all linked as interdependent members of a region
based on work patterns. The following sections detail two important factors that aid our understanding of this region—the urban connection via

Interstate Highway 85 through Cabarrus County and the political incorporation of Kannapolis.

Cabarrus County: Urban Corridor

In order to understand the extent to which the counties have become interdependent and the role Cabarrus County plays, it is important to examine the county itself. As described in Chapter 5, Cabarrus County's prominence in the textile industry began when J. W. Cannon acquired land and started the development of Kannapolis, which was to become the largest mill town in North Carolina. Eventually, Cannon Mills would employ over 20,000 people, and Kannapolis would become the largest producer of consumer textiles in the country. Throughout much of the twentieth century, Cabarrus County was a leader in the industry that dominated the North Carolina economy. The county had an industrial economy that provided jobs for most of its people, and it enjoyed a largely self-contained life. As recently as 1970, 65 percent of all non-agricultural jobs in the county were in textile mills. However, by 1991 that figure had dropped to 29 percent (United States Census of Manufacturing 1992; Stuart 1993).

Cannon Mills, the area's main employer, dominated the economy of Cabarrus County until the recent decades. Then, as the textile industry restructured, the number of workers declined. Following traditional use of the Standard Industry Classification code 2200 to define textile mill employment, data from the North Carolina Employment Security Commission indicate that in 1970, there were 24,720 textile workers in Cabarrus County. In 1980, there were 20,140 textile employees; in 1990, there were 10,640; and in 1992, only 7,695 textile workers remained in the county (United States Bureau of the Census). However, the total employment in Cabarrus County has remained relatively stable, averaging 37,500 workers yearly from 1970 to 1991. The loss of over 12,000 textile jobs in two decades, combined with a steady number of workers in the county, compels further clarification.

Examination of in- and out-migration suggests that an increased number of people have moved into Cabarrus County. Over 9,000 people moved into the county between 1980 and 1990 (North Carolina Employment Security Commission 1992). However, according to interview accounts, some of these newcomers represent people who were drawn to employment opportunities in the Charlotte region but who found living in Cabarrus County to be a desirable alternative to Mecklenburg County (see also Stuart 1993). Thus, new residents of Cabarrus County may commute to other locales for work.

What about the former textile workers? Have they found non-textile employment within their county of residence, or have they joined the out-migration to Charlotte-Mecklenburg? Evidence suggests many people work in new industries that have recently opened in the county. An indicator of the effect of new industry on employment opportunities is the fact that unemployment rates in the county did not rise sharply between 1980 (4.8%) and 1990 (3.8%), despite the drop in textile jobs. Unemployment rates in Cabarrus County did rise during 1982-1986 as Cannon Mills underwent ownership changes, peaking at 8.4% in 1985. By 1987, however, unemployment had leveled out; by 1990, it was actually lower than in 1980. Additionally, average weekly wages in Cabarrus County have risen steadily, an increase brought about in part by the introduction of new industry to the area.

We can also examine the wage structure of employment in Cabarrus County to support the idea that ex-textile workers stayed in the county for jobs. Data from the North Carolina Employment Security Commission (1992) indicate that net job loss occurred in industries paying wages below the state average, such as textiles. Net job gain occurred in manufacturing of "other," a category that contains tobacco products. This group contains the Philip Morris cigarette plant, which opened in 1986, and a higher-than-average wage level is present in the manufacturing group. The addition of those high-wage jobs had a significant effect, causing overall wages to climb relative to the statewide average (see also Stuart 1993).

When the Cannon family owned the mills, no other industry was allowed in the unincorporated region. With the end of Cannon rule, regional industrialization has begun to expand. Philip Morris, one of the major cigarette manufacturers, has a manufacturing plant in the county. Philip Morris pays high wages (relative to textile jobs), and the competition for these jobs is tough. According to one textile-worker informant in 1995, the starting pay at Philip Morris was $14 to $15 per hour, while Fieldcrest Cannon pay started around $7 per hour. Other major employers that have recently entered the area include a prison, a semi-conductor manufacturer, and a poultry plant. These industries have helped maintain Cabarrus County's steady employment despite a significant number of residents who travel to work in the Charlotte-Mecklenburg area.

The influence of Philip Morris on the economic autonomy of Cabarrus County is also evident when examining the value-added measure of manufacturing—a statistical measure of the extent to which the worth of raw materials is increased by processing. Expressing value added on a per capita basis will indicate whether an industry is labor intensive (low value added per employee) or capital intensive (high value added per employee). The textile industry historically has been very labor intensive; this is reflected in the Cabarrus County data for 1977 and 1982, where the value added per worker was $15,915 and $17,648, respectively. These figure are much lower than the national averages of $29,870 in 1977, and $43,191 in 1982 (United States Census of Manufacturing, 1992). The situation changed drastically as of 1987, by which time Philip Morris was in production in its new plant and Fieldcrest Cannon had implemented its modernization program. At that point, the Cabarrus County per-employee figure was $101,905, well above the national average of $61,526 (United States Census of Manufacturing 1992).

Obviously, not everyone in Cabarrus County can work at Philip Morris or in other high-paying jobs in new industry; these realities help explain another example of change in workforce patterns in Cabarrus County: out-commuting. A substantial number of Cabarrus residents work outside the county, and the number of commuters out of Cabarrus County doubled from 8,463 in 1980 to 16,603 in 1990 (North Carolina Employment Security Commission 1992). One community leader informant estimated that in 1996, 20,000 people departed from the county every day for work. Interstate Highway 85, connecting Cabarrus County and surrounding rural communities to the urban center of Charlotte, facilitates the commute. I-85 provides direct access to the Charlotte airport, uptown Charlotte, and to other area business and service centers. The average daily traffic flow for I-85 at the Cabarrus-Mecklenburg County line has increased 43.8 percent from 1983 (24,000) to 1991 (34,500) (North Carolina Employment Security Commission 1992). Near Cabarrus, this "urban corridor" includes the Charlotte Motor Speedway, the Philip Morris plant, and most recently, a Brass Pro Fishing Outlet. As witnessed in field research, these developments were accompanied by a new highway exit ramp, hotel, and gas/convenience store built near I-85 on the outside of Kannapolis.

Population and unemployment rates also substantiate the interdependence of the areas. Cabarrus County had a population of 98,935 in 1990, a 15 percent increase from 1980 (85,895). Cabarrus County's unemployment rate in June 1992 was 6.3 percent. Average weekly wages in 1977, 1986, and 1991 were $156, $299, and $386 respectively, all below the state average (North Carolina Employment Security Commission 1992). The wages for Mecklenburg County, however, are above state average. This fact, combined with the decline in traditional jobs in the county, helps lure many Cabarrus workers to the Charlotte-Mecklenburg region.

By examining social class inequality, we find another indicator of change in the county. Following the measures used by Tomaskovic-Devey and Roscigno (1996), I use the Gini index of inequality in income distribution among households to infer the extent that working-class members lose or gain relative to upper-class members. Researchers compute the index across nine income categories. Theoretically, the value can vary from zero, representing complete equality, to 88.9 (the maximum value when computed across nine income categories), representing complete inequality. In 1980, the Cabarrus County Gini index was 25, a sign of low inequality. In 1990, the index had risen to 32, suggesting that industry moved into the area and paid higher wages (e.g., Philip Morris). The shift in this index becomes meaningful when we compare the family poverty rates for the same period. In 1980, the family poverty rate (for a family of four) in Cabarrus County was 7 percent; in 1990, it was 6 percent. This very slight change is not especially significant, suggesting that part of the increased income inequality occurred at the upper end of the income distribution. The fact that income inequality increased in Cabarrus County despite hardly any decrease in poverty could indicate that higher inequality results from rising wages. In contrast to an economy dominated by relatively equal, low-paying textile jobs, the jobs in the current labor market are polarized. Some of the new jobs (e.g., Philip Morris) pay higher than average wages; others, most likely those in the personal service sector, pay lower than average wages. As such, the degree of inequality is magnified. The findings support the conclusion drawn by Tomaskovic-Devey and Roscigno (1996), that the *type* of local economic development is crucial to inequality in the southern United States. In the Cabarrus County case, the addition of new jobs offering high wages did not result in less inequality.

Interview accounts support the statistical claims. Gale, a social worker in Cabarrus County, reported that Phillip Morris jobs start at $16 to $18 per hour and attract people from both within and outside the county. However, the company hires relatively few workers, meaning that only a small number of residents receive high wages from the new jobs. Others remain unemployed or end up working in low-paying personal service jobs, strengthening the gap between haves and have-nots.

In sum, Cabarrus County is no longer an autonomous area that provides jobs for its residents as it did when Cannon Mills dominated the local labor market and provided a stereotypical "mill village" for its residents. Today, there are some "good," well-paying jobs in the county, but the typical job pays below state and national average wages. At the same time, the population of Cabarrus County has increased. Most of the new residents work outside the county, with many commuting to the Charlotte-Mecklenburg area via the "urban corridor."

Kannapolis, North Carolina: Political Incorporation

The final geographical region to focus on is the community of Kannapolis, located in Cabarrus County. Kannapolis, a 35-minute drive from Charlotte, North Carolina, has a population of 29,696, a 2 percent decrease from the 1980 population of 30,303 (United States Census, 1990). A major employer in Kannapolis is Fieldcrest Cannon, with 6,800 workers in Plant #1 and 400 workers in Plant #4 (North Carolina Department of Commerce 1997). While this change is a significant drop from the 22,000 employed at Cannon Mills in the 1970s, Fieldcrest Cannon remains the dominant employer in Kannapolis. Other employers include Terry Products with 472 workers, Kannapolis Publishing with 46 workers, Lincoln Log Homes with 34 workers, and Hooper Hosiery with 16 workers (North Carolina Department of Commerce 1997).

As discussed earlier, James W. Cannon founded the community of Kannapolis to support his textile mills. It is important to note that Kannapolis remained unincorporated until 1985. Before Murdock's purchase of Cannon Mills, the Cannon family provided all services to Kannapolis. Cannon money supported housing, water, waste, and entertainment services. The Cannons had a reason for maintaining Kannapolis as an unincorporated town—they could control entry of new manufacturers and therefore dominate the local labor market. No major factory other than Cannon Mills existed in Kannapolis until the town's incorporation. For the most part, workers in the area were destined to mill jobs. And Cannon, being the only firm hiring, could dictate pay and benefit levels.

Currently, the incorporated city of Kannapolis supports over 275 community facilities, including churches, local motels, shopping centers, recreation programs, a country club, YMCA, movie theater, library, and a textile museum (field research, 1996; North Carolina Department of Commerce 1997). Kannapolis has six elementary schools, one junior high, and one high school. The nearest community college is the local campus of Rowan-Cabarrus Community College. Several colleges and universities are nearby, including Davidson College, North Carolina–Charlotte, and Barber Scotia. The proximity of higher education facilities is potentially important for ex-textile workers seeking alternative career paths. In addition, industries can use these institutions, especially the community college, to teach new employees necessary skills. For example, several interview respondents (including workers and community development leaders) informed us that Philip Morris had made an agreement with the community college to train its new hires.

Since incorporation, the city has added a local development corporation, a Chamber of Commerce, and an Economic Development Commission. Several key individuals serve on multiple boards, providing the opportunity for networking and concentration of interests. Interviews with members of these organizations demonstrate the importance that local developers place on strategic planning in their efforts to bring new industries to the area; each group espouses a vision statement on future directions for Kannapolis. The visions include expanding the downtown retail area, extending plumbing and sewage, and improving the educational system.

As described in an interview with an informant from the office of city planning, Kannapolis is a "unique" city in that its incorporation is so recent. Kannapolis has its own school system and, though capital poor, has valuable classroom space that Cabarrus Country would like to share. Kannapolis has always had problems with geographical barriers, in particular, watersheds. Current debates revolve around spending money to spread the waterflow out, or reinvesting in the existing infrastructure. The watershed problem is one limit to expansion of development in Kannapolis.

Interview and statistical data show that Kannapolis remains a textile town even though several mills have closed and many jobs have been lost. The Cannon family cultural legacy of paternalism continues to have significant influence among local residents. As one community leader informant described it, the Cannons have "deep pockets" in the community, reinforcing a "legacy of traditionalism and lack of leadership." The same respondent, who worked with economic development, stated, "Leadership is the weakness of the community; it is not a possessed asset." When asked why, the respondent claimed it was a "kickback" to the conditioning of Cannon. The respondent explained that the culture surrounding Cannon is widespread and noted that at one time, even the state of North Carolina was indebted to Cannon.

The lack of leadership and the attitude of dependence were echoed by other community leaders. One, from the county office of economic development, claimed that the unique characteristic of the area is the work ethic created by Cannon, referred to as the "Charlie Cannon phenomenon." The respondent boasted that three generations of people remember "Mr. Charlie." As a result, the respondent claims "Kannapolis leads the nation in terms of labor-force productivity." To this respondent, who has the responsibility of recruiting new industries to the area, the most important selling factor is the productivity and mentality of the established bluecollar labor force.

This raises questions of continuity and change in paternalistic relations (Leiter 1982). Interview accounts suggest a strong attachment to community among some residents and textile workers. There were cases of children and grandchildren staying in town. For example, Emma, a community activist, grew up in Kannapolis and went to a nearby college. Upon graduation, she lived for a period in New York. However, she returned to Kannapolis after a couple of years. When asked why, she states that it is her "home" and she wants to "give back" to the community. However, statements such as this were not the norm. There were also examples of offspring moving out of Kannapolis. Two of Mae's three children (Mae worked as a domestic for the Cannons throughout the mid-1950s, and her husband worked in the mills) had moved to Charlotte and worked in professional occupations. Mae was proud of these children and felt they had "bettered" themselves by leaving Kannapolis.

Although the paternalist culture established by the Cannon family continues to influence local residents, many of whom fondly remember working for Charles Cannon, there is also evidence that cultural ties are being broken. On the one hand, some residents romanticize the previous era—several interview respondents felt that worker relations were best under Cannon and do not demonstrate the same allegiance to current owners. Additionally, new textile workers, such as Hispanics, did not experience the mill village culture. Thus, the best conclusion from my limited data is that Kannapolis is in a state of flux, slowly waning from paternalistic relations. Currently, economic developers may use the "Charlie Cannon phenomenon" to draw new industry to the area on the bases of a deferential, respectful workforce. However, it is quite possible that the phenomenon is fading and the next generations of workers will be less likely to exhibit deference to tradition power (for a thorough discussion of paternalism as social capital, see Schulman and Anderson 1999).

How does the town of Kannapolis relate to its surrounding areas? Kannapolis has an intriguing relationship with the neighboring town of Concord, also located in Cabarrus County. Historically, when the Cannons built the mills, workers lived in Kannapolis, and managers and owners lived in Concord (10 miles away). Residential segregation separated owners and laborers. As the communities grew, they developed separate identities. Rivalry exists between the communities. One of the community leader informants noted that Kannapolis citizens do not trust Concord or Cabarrus County and are adamant about remaining independent. According to one informant, we can trace these attitudes back to early days when mill hands lived in Kannapolis and managers in Concord. Today, the rivalry has resulted in different levels of resources. Concord has expanded with a great deal of annexation. Kannapolis, in an effort to keep up, has attempted to expand, but with little relative success. Respondents frequently noted that Kannapolis has infrastructure problems, including watersheds, zoning, city transportation, and liquor laws, to name a few.

To summarize, three major social consequences have occurred in the nature and organization of the labor market area that includes Cabarrus County and the town of Kannapolis. First, the incorporation of Kannapolis has allowed local industrial expansion. From interviews with economic developers, it is apparent that this continued expansion is a major goal. Second, there have been changes in the jobs in the county. Textile jobs have declined, and others (e.g., poultry, cigarettes) have grown. The decline of textile manufacturing has had consequences for the entire county of Cabarrus. Workers are more likely to commute outside the county for jobs. At the same time, however, new residents are appearing in the county. These trends relate to the third significant change, the inclusion of Cabarrus County in the Charlotte-Mecklenburg County labor market area, which signifies an important change in jobs and commuting-to-work patterns. In 1980, workers in textile jobs dominated the LMA surrounding Kannapolis. In 1990, Kannapolis had become part of an urban metropolitan LMA, and the diversity of employment opportunities increased for Kannapolis residents. Not only did the geography and organization of work change, but the racial composition of the locality also changed during the period under review.

RACE: OLD AND NEW MINORITIES

Race has played a significant role in the development of the textile industry in the southern United States. Before integration efforts in the 1960s, whites did not allow blacks to work in the textile plants, except for a few black men who worked as janitors and bale breakers. Whites often hired black women as domestics and childcare providers. After the Civil Rights legislation of the 1960s, blacks were allowed to work in the mills but were placed in the dirtiest, most difficult and hazardous jobs. As Emma explained,

> The dirty jobs were more people of color, black men. And lint type of jobs. You would go through the plants from the opening room, where they open the bale of cotton (you now have to wear a mask) and progressively, as you went through the mill, it got whiter, and whiter, and whiter and you'd get to the very top, which was clean...it was always white.

In the Kannapolis area, Blacks represent the "old" or established minority, but the overall racial composition of the labor market area has changed over the years. According to 1980 United States Census data, 23.1 percent of the LMA population was black (as defined by 1990 boundaries). There was little change in 1990: 22.6 percent of LMA residents were black. In 1980, only 0.73 percent of residents in the nine-county area were Hispanic. In 1990, the number increased to 9.0 percent. Other racial minority groups represented in the LMA include Laotians, Thai, Vietnamese, and Cambodian.

The introduction of diverse racial groups is part of the process of globalization in its increased international competition for labor and the increased mobility of workers. As Stanley (1994) describes, a dramatic transformation of labor force composition often accompanies industry restructuring. In the meatpacking industry, for example, the number of immigrant and refugee workers and the number of native-born migrant workers has increased since the late 1970s.

Recent statistics show a dramatic change in the size of the Hispanic workforce in Cabarrus County. The 1990 United States Census estimate of Hispanics in Cabarrus County was 483. The 1995 population estimates from social service providers, county activists, and local church leaders suggest the number was at least 3,500. Most Hispanics come to the area for production line jobs (*Charlotte Observer*, September 24, 1995), some migrating from Costa Rica, Guatemala, Mexico, and other Latin American countries; others from national states such as Texas and New Mexico. One community leader informant estimated that at least 400 Hispanics work at a poultry plant in jobs paying minimum wage.

Some Hispanics have moved into jobs in the textile mills, with wages and working conditions that represent a form of upward mobility, even though the jobs for the "new" minority are usually in the packing rooms, the lowest paid jobs in the mill. However, several respondents felt that Hispanic hires are being placed in better jobs and starting at higher wages than those of whites and blacks. For example, Raymond, a retired mill worker, asserted that new hires now receive $7.25 per hour, a figure confirmed in a Kannapolis newspaper advertisement and one that is a significant increase from the $6.00 per hour standard rate at which most whites started before Hispanic immigration. In addition, new Fieldcrest Cannon hires go through a 32- to 36-week training program during which they are not bound to any specific production quota. Interview respondents claim that older hires had a much shorter training period. Raymond, who has been active in unionization struggles, felt the new hiring policy was a company tactic to reverse any possible union drive. By paying workers higher wages and giving longer training periods, the company hopes to show that workers do not need a union.

By employing "new minorities," the company is also building a diverse group of laborers who may be less likely to achieve the solidarity needed to unionize. Fieldcrest Cannon is actively resisting potential unionization. As Raymond said, it appears Fieldcrest Cannon is taking actions to "smother the union." Another informant mentioned that several churches were sponsoring Southeast Asian immigrant workers, singling out one manager's church as having a history of immigrant sponsorship.

Fieldcrest Cannon and Kannapolis are participating in a form of globalization—instead of moving plants to third-world locations, third-world workers have moved to the plants. According to informants, the hiring of new minority workers may be used to pressure existing workers. For example, Lisa, an established employee and known union supporter, was required to train a Hispanic male to do her job. According to Lisa, the worker had no textile experience and understood very little English. As she put it, "I was supposed to train a foreigner to learn something that had taken me 26 years to do." She trained him, however, and tried to teach him everything she knew. The new worker quit after two weeks, saying the job was too difficult for anyone.

The position of new minorities in the labor market today is a reflection of historical discrimination (Bylerly 1986; Fink and Reed 1994; Hall et al. 1987). The potential for prejudice is not surprising given that patterns of racism are embedded in the structure of the labor market. Several of the black respondents provide evidence for embedded racism. James, who grew up in Kannapolis, worked in Plant 8 in China Grove after serving in the Navy. Management had integrated the mills by then and allowed blacks to work. Informally, however, interview accounts note the existence of two pay scales, one for whites and a lesser one for blacks. Furthermore, the firm did not allow blacks on production lines, thus not allowing them to earn extra money. James says this situation gradually changed and blacks are now "more equal" to whites of the same social class.

Mae, a black woman in her 80s, worked for the Cannons as a household servant during the 1940s and 1970s. She spent 6 years in the mills cleaning offices, but returned to domestic work. Her husband, who is now deceased, worked as a janitor in the mills, cleaning bathrooms during the 1940s and 1950s. Mae explains that he was not allowed to drink out of the water fountain, so he had to carry a water bottle. All public places were segregated. Blacks and whites could not use the same bathrooms or eat at the same places. Currently, Mae's daughter and son-in-law, Sue and Will, live next door and work in Fieldcrest Cannon mills. Sue hems wash "rags." She has worked with Cannon for 30 years and was the first black woman to work with machinery in the washcloth room in the late 1960s. Will works in the bleach room, where he takes wet towels to be dried. Will, who is from Concord, started with Cannon in 1952 as a janitor, worked on the cotton platform, then got moved to the bleach room in 1956.

Both Sue and Will benefited from Mae's association with the Cannon family. In the early 1960s, managers asked Mae to recommend a black woman to work in the washroom. Her daughter Sue got a letter the next day. The washroom is relatively clean, and the pay is one of the best for mill jobs. Likewise, after Will married Sue, Mae spoke to Cannon about him and got him moved to the bleach room, where he was one of three black men among many whites. This is also a relatively clean and well-paying job.

Were there tensions between blacks and whites with integration? Sue said no, that management owners had warned the white workers "not to say anything mean." The company held a meeting instructing the whites to accept Blacks. But when Sue describes her first days, her story tells otherwise. When she walked in the room, the whites would stop working and line up against the wall to watch her for 10 minutes or so. She would be "really nervous," and her "stomach would get in knots."

Sue and Will definitely experienced racism. How do they feel about racism and the "new minorities?" In general, both respondents expressed fear of job competition. Their statements suggest misconceptions and inaccuracies, such as Will alleging that the immigrants do not have taxes taken out for five years. Mae, agreeing, added that they do not have to pay taxes on their purchases at Belks (a local department store). Sue said the new immigrants lived in houses of "15 or so" people, and "saved all their money to send back home." Will vouched for a strong work ethic, claiming that these immigrants would "work until you told them to go home." I asked if he thought the new immigrants faced problems similar to blacks during the early days of integration. Sue quickly replied, "Oh no—they can just walk into the jobs. They don't have to overcome obstacles like we [blacks] did."

Emma, a 38-year-old black woman who lived in Kannapolis most of her entire life, is now an organizer for a progressive local grassroots group. She provided poignant examples of the effect of race in the community, recounting a history of segregation in the mills. According to Emma, prior to the 1960s,

> The only place that was integrated was the smoker. There was this particular area that you'd do smoking in. Certain things within the plant that were for men—it was mostly men—to spit in and they had saw dust in them... and smokers, they were these wooden boxes. They were separated by race and gender...had to keep black men and white women separate, you know. But they were side by side.

Emma's experiences at the mill were not all negative. She is careful to point out that there was some economic privilege, especially for workers on production who "were young and fast, and ...could produce." Emma's mother was able to purchase a mill house. In this and other ways, Emma's life differed from those of most blacks. Emma, her siblings, and their mother lived in a house in "the white section of town." So the experience of mill villages was not uniformly negative for blacks, especially when it elevated their standard of living, the case for many after 1964.

In 1996, the organization Emma worked for had two main organizational programs underway. One was geared toward organizing minorities or people who have traditionally been oppressed. The other was aimed at organizing progressive middle-class whites and blacks who did not grow up poor. The goal of both programs was to encourage the development of new leaders for Kannapolis. The groups are structured around issues, such as voter registration, political leadership, and community housing, rather than race, class, or gender-based identities.

The grassroots organization's emphasis on issues rather than on identity is important for a variety of reasons. As noted by John, a union organizer born and raised in Kannapolis, the problems of the area are the result of compounded racism and class inequality. A key example is annexation. According to John, state law requires cities to provide water and sewage to newly annexed areas within a certain amount of time. Nevertheless, Kannapolis officials have not followed the law. On a community tour, John showed me poor neighborhoods where "kids play in sewage in their front yards." One of the sites was in a racially segregated section of town. However, the problem is not limited to black neighborhoods. For example, Kannapolis recently spent a large amount of money on a minor league baseball complex. While the city installed water and sewage at the ball-park, they did not extent amenities to the surrounding neighborhoods where both black and white lower-class people live. To John and many others, this is evidence of both class and race discrimination. John, like Emma, supports programs that focus on issues (i.e., providing water and sewage) rather than racial or class identity. Emma extended the argument to women, noting that sexism also compounds the problem.

Racism continues to exist in the community, although it has become less straightforward. New dynamics, expressed as tensions between "new" and "old" minorities, create complex and fluid situations that are typically compounded by gender and class divisions. Hispanic migration reflects patterns of globalization seen in other United States production localities, including the furniture industry in North Carolina, the meat-packing industry in Nebraska, and hog processing in Iowa. These trends are important keys to understanding contemporary racial (and potentially gender) dynamics as work in the United States expands internationally. As will be argued in the concluding chapter, the globalization of the workforce demands further attention from sociologists.

HOUSEHOLD STRATEGIES

A study of community-level social consequences also needs to involve the mix of livelihood or survival strategies that workers adopt in response to changes in their environment. Survival strategies are diverse conditions and organizational relations that allow human beings to survive and adapt in various social contexts and groups (Mingione 1991). Household strategies are those actions taken by individuals and households of individuals to provide resources for immediate needs and long-term goals (Garrett 1993). Such strategies go beyond survival of individuals in a strict sense, but also include strategies for promoting welfare and potential social mobility. Specific to this case, I expand the definition of household survival strategies to cultural contexts. For example, company owners met many family needs under traditional paternalism (e.g., income, loans, housing, recreation). As will be described, current workers face new dilemmas—care for elderly parents, insufficient income, layoffs and unemployment—without paternalistic benevolence.

Multiple family members working multiple jobs is a common reaction to the current slow economic growth and increased inequality (Danziger and Gottschalk 1995; Sklar 1995). Likewise, in this specific case, all the couples I interviewed were dual-income families. This is not a new pattern for textile workers—the southern textile industry was founded on family labor (Hall et al. 1987). However, the fact that many individuals are working jobs *in addition to* their full-time mill work is an important aspect of workers' lives in Kannapolis. Mill workers also hold jobs at fast food restaurants, grocery stores, and retailers such as Wal-Mart. I interviewed Ned at his produce job in a grocery store where he worked five hours each day after his eight-hour mill shift ended. Increases in living costs, declines in real wages, and the removal of services that mill owners once provided all contribute to increased efforts to improve household resources. Survival strategies might take the form of increased time in the paid labor force, but, as I will show, they also take the form of employment outside the formal labor market.

According to one community leader informant, working families in Kannapolis are close knit and share with each other. Churches play an important role and help with recreation centers, parks, and civic organizations. A different community leader informant, one who worked with the county social services, supports the claim that churches provide much-needed resources. As she noted, none of the social service agencies allow multiple visits from recipients, and the amount of relief a person may get is limited. Some churches offer supplements; many people "double up" (i.e., share with others) and do without things they are used to having.

A serious problem in the area is the lack of housing for low-income residents. According to the social service agency informant, no one is willing to invest in low-rent housing. The few exceptions in 1995 included Habitat for Humanity, which built 15 houses, a HUD affordable housing grant that resulted in 14 houses, and 30 new units of public housing. No doubt, these 59 new houses helped—but the problem remained as 700 people waited on a housing list.

In an interview with a female-male Hispanic couple, the lack of adequate housing demonstrated the prevalence of racial discrimination in the community. According to the informants, for various reasons, many property owners do not want to rent to Hispanics. Others who will rent to Hispanics tend to charge higher rents and provide inadequate maintenance. The situation often leaves many Hispanic families to share a dwelling. According to the female respondent, a particularly "interesting phenomenon" is that single Hispanic mothers will share a house with three or more families in similar situations. The result is "a lot of people living together, maybe seven people in one room...it can destroy a house." Given their inability to pay rent, doubling or tripling up is a survival strategy. Ironically, in contrast to portraying the renters as money conscious, the situation contributed to negative stereotypes of Hispanics.

The Hispanic couple also mentioned that members of their racial group were taking advantage of each other. For example, those that can speak English will often "sell" their abilities to non-English-speaking Hispanics and accompany them to doctors' appointments and legal services. Similarly, Hispanics who have local drivers' licenses and access to cars will sell "taxi" services to other Hispanics who are without transportation. The Hispanic couple was troubled that Hispanics would charge each other for such services and viewed the widespread unwillingness of these newcomers to unconditionally support each other as problematic. Rather than focus on the improvement of Hispanics overall, some enterprising members worked according to American ethics of individual success and independence.

Some of the disabled and retired workers who were out of the mills did odd jobs, like helping neighbors repair cars, renting trailers, and holding yard sales. I witnessed many examples of extended families, with siblings and aunts, grandmothers (and in one case a grandfather) taking active roles in caring for the children. Again, this is common for mill families, given the nature of mill labor (Hall et al. 1987). What differs is that the firm no longer provides community resources to enhance family survival. As interviews suggest, private businesses have replaced company-supported housing, recreation, entertainment, banking, and groceries. While it can be argued this conversion to a "free" market economy removes workers from the paternalistic relations of deference and control, we should remember that all markets are embedded in social contexts and (re)produced by individual actors (Granovetter 1992). Our current post-Fordist economy serves to benefit few at the expense of many. The demise of company obligations contributing to the survival of mill families accompanied the escape of textile workers from paternalist control into the "freedom" of the modern marketplace (Schulman and Anderson 1999). At the same time, state and federal government have failed to effectively take up the company's obligations.

CONCLUSION: NEW WINNERS, NEW LOSERS

Restructuring, globalization, and spatialization have redefined the labor market in general and the specific area around Fieldcrest Cannon mills. Kannapolis has transformed from an isolated, insular community governed by paternalism to a community integrated into a complex regional network of jobs, housing, and commuting. On one hand, the end of a tightly controlled labor market should benefit workers by providing a variety of employment opportunities. On the other hand, the paternalistic community services provided by the dominant firm no longer exist. Because of mergers, closings, and automation, fewer textile jobs exist; but a greater number of job alternatives have developed in the local labor market area. For some, manufacturing jobs in Cabarrus County provide higher wages. For others, however, jobs in the immediate area paying below national averages are the alternative. While opportunities for better jobs exist in the Charlotte-Mecklenburg region, they are only available to those with a means of transportation.

Poverty rates in Cabarrus County have remained stable, but inequality has increased. The racial composition of the area is changing—no longer are southern race relations restricted to black-white dynamics. Many problems remain for the Kannapolis area. Community leader informants continuously cited lack of leadership and solidarity as significant drawbacks for residents. In addition, social services are inadequate to meet the needs of poor families. Schools, hospitals, and law enforcement are poorly prepared to handle the influx of Spanish-speaking immigrants. There is no public transportation in Kannapolis, in Cabarrus County, or along the urban corridor to Charlotte.

Overall, have these changes been positive or negative for the community of Kannapolis? This is a difficult question to answer and might be best rephrased in terms of "winners" and "losers." For some the change is positive, especially for those who are able to commute to better jobs in Charlotte, or for those whose move to Cabarrus County is a step up (i.e., Hispanics), or for those employed in the new local high-wage jobs. For others the change is negative, such as for those who had to relinquish mill jobs and retirement benefits during the downsizing, merging, and pension-raiding of Cannon Mills. Consistent with other research (i.e., Bluestone and Harrison 1982; Harrison and Bluestone 1988; Fitchen 1991, 1995; Johnson 1990), the processes of globalization, restructuring, and spatialization definitely have negative impacts for some community members of Kannapolis and Cabarrus County. Inequality in the community has increased, supporting the widening gap between haves and have-nots.

However, researchers must avoid considering the social consequences as dichotomous or all-inclusive. The outcomes of restructuring, spatialization, and globalization are producing a mixed bag of effects. Employment opportunities prevail for some community members and diminish for others. The changing social processes create new opportunities for some people, but are also accompanied by increasing unemployment, poverty, and earnings inequality that affect many others.

Processes of change in the community continue to occur unevenly, affecting individuals in various ways. Indeed, economic restructuring has modified the structure of power and domination in this southern textile community. Perhaps it is ironic that the dismantling of paternalism has resulted in many negative consequences in terms of the daily life of community members. Ideally, the restructuring of the labor market should provide greater opportunities for workers. Nevertheless, this is not necessarily the case. As seen here, the "free" market is embedded in complex social relations, including historical and modern pressures. The social consequences of change for Kannapolis are embedded in previous sets of social relations, perhaps the most significant being paternalism. In Kannapolis, emerging forms of social organization are rooted within industry, national, and global contexts. As will be expanded in the concluding chapter, the new structures are created and serve to maintain class-based, racial, and gendered divisions and serve as global-local linkages.

Chapter Seven
Workplace Outcomes
Remaking the Labor Process

I continue the analyses of the social impacts of change in this chapter, expanding the focus from the community to the workplace. Given the fact that impacts in the community occur unevenly, can we expect the processes of globalization, restructuring, and spatialization to have similar effects on the shopfloor? As discussed in Chapters Three and Four, global competition has compelled firms within the United States textile-mill complex to develop a new retail orientation that emphasizes quality control and quick response to changing market conditions (Bonham 1991). But new technologies are not neutral—they can have both negative and positive consequences for workers on the shopfloor.

The classical argument about the effect of change brought on by workplace technology can be found in the work of Braverman (1974), who argued that with bureaucratization, increased standardization, and technological innovation, workers are being deskilled as mental and physical labor are increasingly separated. That is, managers are increasingly in charge of the conceptualization and planning process, while workers are merely used for the power of their physical labor. Another important scholar is Blauner (1964), who focused on issues of workplace autonomy and alienation and contended that some production technologies create a sense of powerlessness, meaninglessness, isolation, and self-estrangement among workers.

Edwards (1979) examines the history of industrial control under capitalism and demonstrates the existence of three forms of control: simple, technical, and bureaucratic. Each form of control developed in response to the contradictions inherent within the former system. Thus, simple entrepreneurial control was succeeded by simple hierarchical control, and that, in turn, was succeeded by technical control, which then gave rise to bureaucratic control in the post-World War II period. Edwards does not argue that each control is fully replaced by the new form. Instead, previous forms survive as remnants, located in particular sectors, but their dominance is curtailed in favor of the later form.

Focusing specifically on the power or leverage of workers, studies have shown that a number of factors utilized by capitalists in order to boost profit have had the consequence of depressing social welfare and undermining the power and bargaining position of labor. Scholars recount the demise of mass production technology and development of "flexible specialization" (e.g., Harrison and Bluestone 1988; Piore and Sabel 1984). Research suggests that changes in firm and industry structure will affect the workplace and shopfloor labor processes through increased production pace, new management strategies, and technological adjustments (e.g., Grant and Hutchinson 1996; Massey and Meegan 1985; Stanley 1994; Vallas 1993; Vallas and Beck 1996).

For example, new information technologies have transformed the structure of production, making it better suited to respond to rapid and volatile changes in consumption patterns. As competition increases and expands to an international level, firms restructure production in ways that cut costs and increase efficiency. A partial list of examples would include automation, computerization, job cuts, increased job tasks, teamwork, and flexible production techniques such as Just-In-Time (JIT) and Quick Response (QR). Many of these changes are evident in the textile industry (Finnie 1990). The purpose of this chapter is to assess the following question: How have changes in the United States textile-mill complex, specifically at Fieldcrest Cannon, impacted the workplace and workers? Has the remaking of the labor process advantaged or disadvantaged workers on the shopfloor? The answers that emerge center around three decisive shifts: redefining jobs, teamwork, and unsteady employment. In the following pages, I describe these changes and analyze their effects on the structure and culture of shopfloor life in the mills of Fieldcrest Cannon.

REDEFINING JOBS: AUTOMATION AND INCREASED RESPONSIBILITY

The production of textiles is becoming increasingly automated as manufacturers shift toward continuous processing that enables them to respond quickly to market demand. The NCSU textile professors and the company vice-president spoke of a "brave new world of technology," consisting of sophisticated equipment designed to make production more efficient and effective. One example is the "mini-mill" housed at North Carolina State University College of Textiles. In coordination with the private textile corporation, TC^2, the university has produced a demonstration model of the fully automated mill. Computer-aided machinery is the top floor, while the mill operates below, independent of human labor but visible to controllers.

What exactly does automation do to the production process? In general, the production process is shortened as non-value-added steps are removed. A simple example, as seen on a plant tour, involves doffing. Doffing, or unloading yarn and then moving it into another room, has been replaced by automatic transport systems that do not require human labor. With automation, not only are fewer workers needed, but the remaining workers are accountable for multiple jobs as well as increased responsibilities and production demands.

James, a black man around 40 years old who worked in the sewing room of Plant 8 when Murdock purchased the mills in 1984, provided information about changes on the shopfloor. Gradually, as new machines were brought in, jobs were eliminated, and many of James' co-workers were replaced. James stated jobs previously requiring 100 workers could now be done with only 15 workers and that those 15 "had more work to get done." During this period of restructuring, James grew increasingly frustrated with management's use of "scare tactics" and eventually walked off the job in 1988. James now works for the Department of Corrections in the newly constructed prison.

Another example of the effects of automation comes from Raymond, who began working for Cannon in 1943 and is now retired. Raymond worked 43 years in the packing room and vividly recounts the change from hand to automated machinery for taping packages. Initially, workers would strap tape on the packages by hand. Then came the automatic strapper...and after that, an *improved* automatic strapper. Raymond notes that the progress got to the point where "workers didn't have to tape at all—they just placed the package in the correct start position and the machine took over." Raymond is quick to point out that automation did not necessarily improve workers' conditions. While automation lessened physical demands, it created increased production demands. Workers were required to complete a greater number of tasks in a shorter period. As management expectations elevated and workloads were increased, emotional stress increased for workers such as Raymond.

Diane, a white woman who had 25 years in the mills, spoke of changes in shopfloor conditions for clerks. In the past, the sole responsibility of clerks was making orders and overseeing the placement of goods on trucks for distribution. Today, clerks are also required to weigh the goods and physically take them to packing. Doffers no longer carry the goods. Management now expects clerks to complete up to 100 orders per night—a dramatic increase from previous expectations of 20 to 30 orders per night.

Even workers still on production (i.e., those who get paid a base rate with extra pay for pieces that exceed the base) have experienced changes in the nature of their jobs. Sue, the hemmer, reported that managers no longer measure washcloths by the pound. A computerized bar code system now keeps track of how many the worker completes. Sue's job has become more difficult as global trade regulations (see Chapter Three) require workers to sew multiple labels with language translations on the cloths. Additionally, as described in Chapter Four, production is based on retail demand. As consumer tastes change, retailers require a variety of cloth styles. For example, washcloths are becoming larger and thicker. This causes problems for production workers who are expected to hem cloths at a steady rate regardless of size. As Sue reported, it takes longer to hem the bigger washcloths, and workers' production rates decline when faced with this challenge.

Not all workers reported entirely negative feelings about automation, however. Some talked of technology as a mixed blessing. Diane, who had worked in the mills for 25 years, is an automatic winder in the spinning room of Plant 1. She spoke fondly of open-ended spinning, saying it was "fantastic" and she "loved it." According to Diane, the newer, automatic open-ended spinners require less maintenance than previous spinners. Winders like Diane receive cans of roving (the container of cotton strands wound onto bobbins) from the carding room. Before the company installed the new spinners, workers had to insert the bobbins into the spinning machines and then doff (remove) them when they were full of yarn. With automation, "all you have to do is make sure the cans of roving don't run out." The automation does away with the insertion of bobbins, a step that required detailed attention and labor from workers. It also eliminates much of the physical labor involved with moving the cans. Diane described the new, automated process as "beautiful," using gestures that underscore her enthusiasm to describe the job.

We should not interpret Diane's appreciation for the new technology as whole-hearted support for it, however. She noted that shifts have now changed to twelve hours (see next section) and that management assigns spinners more frames to tend. Once a machine gets full, the worker must doff them (remove the cans), or else the warps fall to the floor. The doffing she refers to used to be a separate job assignment performed by specialized workers who removed the roving when the cans were full. Today, spinners themselves must doff the machines. Additionally, the number of machines maintained per worker has increased. According to Diane, "they have stretched it out...so many frames...it is too much to do."

The organization and type of work shifts have changed also. Traditionally, Fieldcrest Cannon ran three eight-hour shifts in its spinning and weaving plants. Currently, they are running two twelve-hour shifts in some of the newer continuous processing spinning and weaving plants. Julie works in the weave room of one of these plants. She works four days in a row, has two days off, works five days, then two off. During her shift, Julie is responsible for making sure that all the looms keep running. She "pulls threads" when they break, "walks her warps" every 15 minutes to keep the trash out, inspects the cloth every two hours, and "flags a loom" if it stops running so a fixer will come repair it. Julie claims that an end (i.e., thread) breaks every 20 seconds and that she may have to restart 40 looms in an hour. She has had as many as 700 stops in a twelve-hour shift. Weavers like Julie spend all twelve hours of the shift on their feet walking cement floors and do not get breaks. Julie complains that the management does not consider this "overworking," but adds, "they're not out there working—we are."

The general automation of the production process in the spinning and weaving plants has contributed to a decline in the number of workers. Ely, a white man in his fifties who had to leave the mill because of brown lung disease, explained that fewer workers were doing production. Today, a fraction ("one tenth") of workers are used to produce the same amount of cloth. According to Ely, the spinning room in Plant 16 went from 308 to 43 workers when David Murdock purchased Cannon Mills. Concurrently, production increased. Ely, like Linda, claims that work is harder for those left in the mills. For example, a doffer (someone who worked in spinning room and exchanged spindles) previously would do two rounds on 19 frames and then take a break while the spindles were re-filling. The doffer could sit down, rest, and wait for the spindles to fill. Now, because machines control the rate of production, the doffer works the entire time without breaks (in some plants the job of doffing itself no longer exists).

While the above comments indicate that technological change and automation are transforming the workplace, researchers should not take them to mean that the transformation is occurring evenly. In general, most firms lack the capital to finance a complete overhaul, making the "lights out," totally automated mill an unrealistic option. Instead, firms install computer-integrated manufacturing systems in stages. For example, on a tour of the shopfloor in one Fieldcrest Cannon mill, the unevenness of technological restructuring was evident. The front end of the plant, containing the first steps in preparing cotton fiber for spinning into yarn, was extremely automated. Machines opened compressed bales of raw cotton and removed dirt and plant debris. The stage of cleaning and sorting, previously one of the dustiest jobs in the plant, now requires very little human labor.

At other stages of production, transformation toward automation was also mixed. In the weaving room, for example, modern looms ran beside older ones. The speed of new looms was visibly faster than the older ones, which appeared to chug along. New looms also require less attention from workers. According to workers, old looms break down frequently, and workers tending these machines have to depend on loom fixers (men who made adjustments, replaced broken parts, and overhaul looms). From the tour it was clear that significant parts of production still rely upon traditional labor processes and old technology. Managers showed us 60-year-old machines in operation beside new machines. Thus, not only is the degree of technological change inconsistent across firms, but it also varies within a single plant.

As production becomes more flexible, continuous, and automatic, traditional means of controlling workers change. As one textile professor noted, company owners no longer need to own mill villages or provide services. The increased production rates, combined with a tight labor market (e.g., relatively high unemployment rates), serve to keep workers on company schedules. If the workers at Fieldcrest Cannon do not want to do their jobs, others (e.g., the new minorities) wait to replace them.

Traditional paternalistic methods of control, which required a significant investment of time and energy for owners, is giving way to market-based, technical, and bureaucratic forms of control. Formal rules, management's use of machines to dictate production, and competition for jobs have replaced informal, personalized attitudes of care and deference (Leiter 1982). At the same time, these factors increase the firm's productive efficiency and help ensure the firm will remain competitive in the expanding textile industry.

The decline of paternalism is evident in workers' descriptions of shopfloor changes under Murdock and Fieldcrest. Established workers claimed the new owners were not interested in the welfare of workers to the same extent that Cannon was. One noted, "Murdock didn't give a flip about us...and we're the ones who keep this place running." Another interviewee noted that although Charles Cannon, the "daddy of the town," ruled with a firm hand, he would listen to workers' complaints. The same did not hold true for Murdock, whom you could complain to "only if you can find the main office." The respondent continued to explain that the situation worsened with Fieldcrest, noting a popular joke that a worker would have to "walk to Eden," where the company's headquarters are located, to complain. Nevertheless, changes in the form of control do not necessarily occur in clean, linear steps (Edwards 1979). As discussed in the previous chapter, the decline of paternalism did not sever all traditional ties between workers and management. Nor did shifts toward technical and bureaucratic control occur *in toto*. Rather, elements of each have been present on the shopfloor in varying degrees throughout the history of the firm.

One informant, a white female in her 50s who had worked in Plant 6 for 19 years, recounts that as the company introduced new machines in the hemming and sewing rooms, older female workers were often unable to push the stiff, heavy towels through them. Some of these women were only one or two years away from retirement when they were faced with changes in technology. Most refused to quit, needing the income and potential retirement benefits. Several respondents complained that it was unfair of Murdock to do this to women who had given their lives to the mills, alluding to the fact that Cannon would not have treated workers in this manner.

Several respondents noted that older workers had higher levels of tolerance for harsh mill working conditions than younger workers. Diane said that older workers are the only ones who are staying with Fieldcrest Cannon. People in their 20s may work for a year or two, but usually quit and seek less demanding jobs. Julie adds that there is great turnover on the twelve-hour shifts. She stated, "It used to be hard to get jobs in the mills. Now young people don't stay because they say the work is too hard." Julie claims the company may hire as many as 200 new workers a month and have only 10 stay. Most of the long-term employees have been at their jobs for 10 to 15 years. On Julie's shift, only two have been there less than 15 years. The more experience workers acquire, the less likely they are to leave. Retirement and health benefits, although minimal, along with fact that age discrimination reduces other employment opportunities, contribute to older workers' limited alternatives outside the mill. Thus, we should not attribute older workers' tolerance for harsh conditions solely to personal endurance. Rather, the limited alternatives they face play an extremely significant role in remaining in mill jobs.

In sum, as new technology invaded the shopfloor, jobs were redefined in ways that typically increased worker responsibility. At times, the changes decreased the physical demands upon workers. However, augmented production requirements and fear of losing one's job to automation may outweigh potential benefits. Concurrently, forms of control shifted away from traditional paternalism toward both technical and bureaucratic control. The result is that workers like Diane, Raymond, James, and Julie must adjust to increases in production pace, new management strategies, and technological adjustments. As the next section demonstrates, management does not leave worker adjustment to individualized, rational choice. Rather, incentives for change are embedded in the new forms of production and strategies of control.

TEAMWORK, MODULES, AND THE DEMISE OF PRODUCTION-BASED PAY

According to one textile professor, production incentives for employees (e.g., extra pay per individual) have given way to team incentives. In modern mills, quality of products is maintained through technology rather than workers' skills. This respondent noted that the textile jobs of today require different skills than previous eras because technology, not individual skills, sets the work method and pace. In many cases, it is useful to have teams of workers. Operators, for example, are only active when the machines break or are full. Then they must stop the machine, which interrupts production. For efficiency, management wants the stops as short and fast as possible. Teamwork is helpful because several workers can get a machine up and running again faster than one person can.

As the need for traditional skills declines, employers are emphasizing new skills, such as literacy, training in quality control, teamwork, and the ability to communicate. At Fieldcrest Cannon, workers are often required to spend time in one of the company's learning centers. During a plant tour, our guides showed us the learning center. A worker can learn English or complete OSHA training regulations on a personal computer with interactive software. Workers can review company policies and information systems in interactive videos. Workers who are not literate can learn basic reading and writing skills. Workers also use the center to learn about new mill equipment. For example, the Japanese company Sudacoma, which produces new looms for Fieldcrest Cannon, provides interactive video training programs to help workers understand operations.

According to one company executive, learning centers are now necessary parts of the textile production. The equipment used in textile production is increasingly sophisticated, and workers need training to operate the machines and keep their skills up to date. The executive acknowledged that the plant's learning center makes the employee better trained primarily for Fieldcrest Cannon. However, he stated that workers have to be prepared to be competitive in the labor market in the event that the textile industry no longer needs them. As such, he sees the learning centers providing "life skills" (e.g., reading) to employees who may one day be out of a textile job.

In a way, the executive's statements reflect a form of self-serving paternalism—the firm, in caring for its workers, wants workers to be able to get alternative jobs in the event that the company can no longer "care" (i.e., employ) for them. The flip side of this sentiment, however, is that the company may be preparing to cut all ties and responsibilities to the local workforce as fewer and fewer textile workers are necessary. Additionally, while not acknowledged by the executive, workers who wish to participate in the learning center must do so on their own time. As such, it is questionable whether the learning centers are incentives or pacifiers for the workforce. New technology allows for less learning on the shopfloor, such as transference of traditional skills between workers. New labor force entrants may come from non-textile backgrounds and therefore must receive comprehensive instruction to operate new equipment.

Traditionally, one form of worker incentive has been increased pay for more work. Ned, a slasher-tender in the cutting room with 40 years of experience (the job of a slasher-tender is to separate the rolls of fabric into batches to be hemmed), provides an example. Before technological changes in the labor process, when a worker was absent, two other workers had the option of taking over the absent worker's job and production rate and splitting the extra pay. With the new technology and the shift to hourly wages, however, this is no longer possible for workers like Ned. If someone is absent, management expects Ned to pick up the extra work; but under the new arrangement, Ned will not receive bonus pay. Because Ned's work is not production driven, management does not give incentives for increased productivity. Technology determines the work pace. Over-production becomes a standard part of the job description rather than an opportunity for increased income.

Some of the textile workers we interviewed are still on production wages; management determines their pay by the amount of work done or pieces produced. Several respondents reported that when a production worker gets ahead (i.e., they exceed base rates), management changes the work pace to slow her/him down. For example, Julie, a weaver who runs between 28 and 30 looms during her twelve-hour shift, gets paid $8.64 per hour as base rate plus 120% of her job performance rate, for a total of $9.60 per hour. If she works over production, she makes $10.40 an hour. However, that wage is almost equivalent to what the firm traditionally considered appropriate for a skilled job such as loom fixers (her husband, a fixer in the same plant, makes $11.64 per hour), and "fixers are supposed to make more than weavers." So one of Julie's looms will be stopped by management "for maintenance" when her production is too high.

With automation, the firm is able to determine the pace of production by machinery. Likewise, the quality of products is maintained by technology, not by workers. Textile firms not longer need traditional knowledge and skills on the shopfloor, as workers are now responsible for monitoring the *equipment* rather than the actual *product*. Incentives for producing beyond quota are becoming less relevant. With new production strategies and a supply of labor, management is no longer required to provide traditional incentives. In many cases, established workers are "aged out" (via retirement or firing) as traditional skills become unnecessary. Today, management prefers literate workers they can train to operate the new equipment.

In addition to trainable workers, management desires employees who have the ability to communicate and work in teams. Like other firms, Fieldcrest Cannon is moving toward the concept of teamwork. According to respondents, the newest machines on the shop floor are in the hemming department of towel manufacturing plants. Workers referred to these machines as modules. Modules perform the multiple functions of hemming, cutting, and sewing. Lisa described how she learned to run the module. According to her, what used to take four or five people to accomplish is now done by one person on new "ergonomic machines." Lisa reported that in the beginning, there were many mistakes as workers learned to operate the modules. Over time, mistakes have lessened. The significance for the workers lies in the switch to "being a team player." In Lisa's department, the team has to "maintain percentage," or produce a certain number of cloths, to make hourly wage. If they fail to meet this goal, management will "write up" team members, labeling them inefficient.

The idea of "team spirit" is dramatically different from individual specialization and is hard for some workers to embrace. Lisa noted that many hemmers switched jobs instead of going to the modules. Workers believe the company is very serious about the team concept. According to interview informants, Fieldcrest Cannon has fired employees for not complying with team organization. Additionally, workers are required to complete classes on dispute management and attend periodic review sessions.

Working with modules requires the employee to be able to do everything, including fix the machines. For the team concept to work efficiently, traditional fixers have to be able to hem. Lisa laughed and said "fixers don't like this and will threaten to quit." On the shopfloor, jobs of hemming are characterized as feminine, while fixing is a masculine job. Will the team concept break down gender boundaries? Or will workers rebel and refuse to participate? As suggested by Lisa, most workers will conform to team expectations because they value continued employment.

Diane expressed another problem with the team concept. In packing, four people work together on a line. The job is still paid on a production basis, and workers can only make "good money" if they work together. Diane reports that the job, which is one of the lowest paid in the company, has a great deal of turnover. "Sometimes you'll have two experienced packers teamed with two new ones...the new ones can't keep up, and the others have to do all the work."

Julie, a weaver, adamantly stated that the team concept would not work. She cited an example where the company dissolved two fixing jobs to put the fixers on the team concept. Fixers, usually male workers who attend to looms, make adjustments, replace broken parts, and conduct general overhauls, now work together and have to cover for each other rather than work independently. Julie's husband is a fixer. Before the team concept, he took care of 97 looms. Now, he works on 130 with no increase in pay. If a team member takes a break or is sick, the remaining ones have to cover for her/him. This also creates a problem for weavers. Fixers are "so scattered about that they don't see the flags" signaling a broken machine. Weavers must leave their looms to find a fixer. They may have to wait three or four hours for the fixer to repair their loom. As Julie noted, during this time the weaver is not meeting production quota. As weavers fall behind, floor managers write them up and cut their wages.

Julie said management plans to move the weavers to the team concept, but she does not like the idea. Currently, weavers have "relief weavers" whose job is to give each weaver a 15-minute break per shift. However, according to Julie, that only happens if all weavers are present—if anyone is sick or absent, the relief weaver takes over her/his loom. As such, Julie reports that often weavers do not get any breaks and must even eat lunch standing up and working.

The issue of breaks is sensitive for current workers. When they first went on the twelve-hour shift, Julie claims the company promised the weavers three 20-minute breaks per shift. Julie said that lasted about 6 months.

Since then (and for the last 6-7 years) the weavers "get a break when there's someone there to give you one," either a relief weaver (when all weavers are present) or a "good" supervisor who is willing to watch the looms long enough for the weaver to take a break. "It's our responsibility to keep the looms running and fixed and make production." The management "cuts points" if weavers do not make production and cuts points if they make over production. That is, weavers must maintain a consistent production pace determined by quota rates. She said if weavers do not meet order deadlines, or if they produce poor quality, Fieldcrest Cannon will lose the order. But the company does not appear to recognize what Julie claims—that the quality is worse with the team approach because of speed-ups.

Julie gave evidence of poor performance caused by forcing workers into teams. For example, management will team up two "good" weavers with a "smoker" (i.e., someone who smokes tobacco products). This causes tension among the workers. The two good weavers will have to cover for the smoker when he/she goes outside for a cigarette break. Julie claims this happens "every 15 minutes" and "we resent doing her work." It is also problematic when an entire team is not present. Snow days are the worst, and "any weaver who comes in to work ends up running a whole section of 100 or more looms."

For Julie, another problem with the team concept is that the company uses it as a way to cut pay. Weavers, whose "official" base pay is $9.40 to $10.40 per hour, end up making less than $9 per hour on a team. According to Julie, the wage of a weaver is directly related to that of a fixer. "Weavers are not supposed to make more than fixers even though they work harder...sometimes fixers only have to fix three looms in a day, so they get more breaks than weavers. Still they make more." Julie explains that the difference is supposedly because "they [the company] have [invested] more time in a fixer." However, as noted earlier, weavers tend to be women, and fixers tend to be men. As numerous researchers report, jobs dominated by men pay more than jobs dominated by women (Tomaskovic-Devey 1993).

In sum, the introduction of modules and the shift toward teamwork presents workers with new challenges. To earn extra money, team members must get along and work at a similar pace with each other. Nevertheless, workers have no discretion in determining their team's work pace. The form of control embedded on the shopfloor is both technological and bureaucratic. Management assembles teams of workers with varying degrees of experience and differing work habits. The team concept still requires a degree of collaboration and support among an increasingly heterogeneous workforce. Management can rely on some degree of social solidarity among workers. However, it is difficult if not impossible for workers to produce beyond a pre-determined rate. Additionally, when a machine breaks down, teams still require attention from fixers. If fixers are unavailable (usually due to overload), the team's production (and thereby earnings) stops. The next section addresses problems that result from inconsistent production.

UNSTEADY EMPLOYMENT: MACHINE BREAKDOWNS, LAYOFFS, AND ALTERNATING SHIFTS

The introduction of teamwork is not the only problem Fieldcrest Cannon employees face. The issue of machine reliability appeared repeatedly in interviews with shopfloor workers. Lisa, in the hemming department, claims the newer hemming machines "don't run worth a flip." The new machines cost more and result in more seconds, more "re-dos" and more "mess" around the shop floor. Rachel notes that production workers, especially fixers, cannot properly maintain the machines. The fixers will "mickey-mouse" them, or use inferior parts to "scotch tape" the machines. Diane supports the fact that new machines are problematic. Although the plant she works in is "one of the most modern plants in the world," they [the fixers] "can't keep them running...they break down a lot." Diane believes that because the new machines are computerized, there are no qualified people to fix them. "Fieldcrest Cannon won't pay qualified people enough to work...so the machines stay broke down half the time."

Sometimes raw materials contribute to a breakdown. Julie, a spinner, complained about imported yarn from Egypt, saying, "This is a textile state. When they go overseas, they are cutting lots of people in this state out of jobs. And that yarn from Egypt won't always run." Another respondent reinforced Julie's frustration, explaining that the Egyptian yarn breaks easily, causing more stops in production. Both strongly felt that the imported yarn results in poorer quality products. The purchase of yarn from Egypt is an example of global sourcing. Companies are no longer relying on local markets for supplies. With globalization and increased competition, products can often be obtain from international markets for less cost.

Machine breakdowns may cause workers to miss production quotas and result in irregular earnings. As Diane notes, when machines break down, she and co-workers must "do odd jobs, if there is any, or get sent home." Diane complains, "We never know what the schedule will be...we can't plan for things 'cause we don't know if we'll have to work." The unreliability also occurs in the form of increased work hours. When a large order is due, the firm will demand more hours from workers. For example, Sue began our interview saying she was tired because she had "been working the 10-hour shifts seven days a week to do a big order from Wal-Mart." This may be a welcome relief for some workers, such as Julie's husband, who desires overtime.

Because the retail market drives production, the firm often dismisses workers and temporarily shuts down plants during periods of low demand. Unsteady work creates multiple problems, one being unreliable income.

However, unsteady work results from other factors in addition to machine breakdowns and layoffs. The firm also alternates shift schedules, often making life for twelve-hour shift workers difficult. Julie, for example, now works four twelve-hour days, followed by three days off, then three twelve-hour days followed by two days off. Sometimes this means she has weekends off; other times she does not. Every few weeks, management rotates Julie and other workers to the opposite shift ("so nobody gets stuck on nights"), and Julie must adjust her sleep schedule. Julie considers herself lucky, despite new shift demands, because she has a husband to help with household responsibilities. New schedules such as the twelve-hour shift put pressure on families, especially those raising children, in their efforts to maintain households.

It was extremely difficult to schedule an interview with a twelve-hour shift worker because of their rotating schedules and need to "squeeze everything—including sleep—into days off." I spent several months before securing the interview with Julie. She was a member of the "sandwich generation" and took care of her mother-in-law, two sons, and, at times, her husband. During the interview, Julie continually expressed discontent over the twelve-hour shifts, blaming it for the behavior problems of her older son, who was a high school dropout and had been in trouble with the law. She said angrily, "You [Fieldcrest Cannon] destroyed my family life with the twelve-hour shift." She said she sees her kids only 24 hours in a week, missing ball games and school functions. She sees them from about 6-6:30 in the morning, long enough to feed them and see the younger son off to the school bus, and then again after 7 p.m., long enough to feed them again and get ready for bed. Julie said the twelve-hour shift is harder on the kids than the eight-hour shift. The parents are unable to go to ball games, coach, or volunteer at the school. There are many kids in "lockkey homes" now. The grocery bill is "way up" now because she has to buy "microwave stuff they can fix for supper." Alternatively, she has to cook extra on her days off. They cannot have the extended family dinners they used to have unless everybody is laid off. At the time of our interview, Julie said she and her husband "don't know whether to buy Christmas or not because we don't know whether we'll have a job in January."

In sum, interruptions in production make life unstable for textile workers on both a day-to-day basis (i.e., machine breakdowns) as well as a larger issue of employment status (i.e., layoffs). New schedules, such as twelve-hour shifts, challenge families to adjust survival strategies and increase the amount of stress for workers like Julie. Current changes are embedded in the emerging retail markets and reflect fluctuations in consumer tastes. A firm's potential for outsourcing and relocation of plants requires workers desiring textile jobs to adapt. Labor market conditions, including the lack of alternative jobs, reinforce the need for many workers to maintain their textile jobs.

CONCLUSION: NEW WINNERS, NEW LOSERS

This chapter has explored the transformation of work under global economic restructuring. As suggested by many scholars, changes in firm and industry structure such as increased production pace, new management strategies, and technological adjustment, impact the workplace and shopfloor labor processes (Grant and Hutchinson 1996; Harrison and Bluestone 1988; Piore and Sabel 1984; Stanley 1994; Vallas and Beck 1996). At Fieldcrest Cannon, bureaucratization and increasing standardization have resulted in the deskilling of labor (Braverman 1974), but only to a partial extent. In many instances, old skills, such as those used by loom fixers, remain indispensable. At the same time, new skills such as literacy and ability to communicate are required. Management has altered existing forms of control, primarily through automation and implementation of the team concept. However, according to Edwards (1979), transformations of control do not require absolution of previous forms. From interviewing workers at Fieldcrest Cannon, it is evident that various forms of control, including paternal (simple), technical, and bureaucratic, often overlap and reinforce one another.

Has the remaking of the labor process advantaged or disadvantaged workers on the shopfloor? Interview evidence suggests both. Millwork has improved in many ways. Plants are not as dirty and dangerous as they were before the industry restructuring of the 1980s. Nevertheless, workers complain about stressful demands, such as increased production rates and coordination of team members, and lack of company loyalty. Indeed, for those workers who were fired or forced out of jobs, automation of the labor process has been negative. For workers remaining in the mills, the new technology may be "fascinating" (as Diane describes it), but also demanding of workers. The complexity of new technology requires different skills from workers. Learning centers facilitate the education of workers, exposing them to new skills and techniques. At the same time, the upgrading of production methods serves to deskill some workers. Firms no longer rely solely on traditional forms of knowledge about textile production. As a result, workers no longer have control over quality; technology is now solely responsible for quality. As Braverman stated 25 years ago,

> The breakup of craft skills and the reconstruction of production as a collective or social process have destroyed the traditional concept of skill and opened up only one way for mastery over labor processes to develop: in and through scientific, technical and engineering knowledge (1974:443).

While Braverman's deskilling thesis generally refers to a much earlier transformation of labor (i.e., initial capitalist attack on craft work), the basic tenets are relevant to this case. Traditional textile labor, with cultural roots in paternalism, is relatively devalued in modern textile mills. As firms continue modernization, we can expect the need for such skills to diminish completely. Ultimately, control of the labor process rests with firm owners.

Perhaps what is unique to this case is how these changes parallel the decline of paternalism. To a certain extent, bureaucratic rules have replaced traditional forms of control in textile mills (Leiter 1982). In the case of Fieldcrest Cannon, management now conveys bureaucratic rules using concepts of "teamwork" and "cooperation" among workers. This form of control, however, is embedded in a market economy that emphasizes profits over people. The ideal image of teamwork is perhaps unattainable, especially as changes in the organization of the labor market and nature of jobs increase racial and skill divisions on the shopfloor. This fact should remind us that new technologies and management strategies are not neutral and ultimately serve to benefit capitalists.

It is also important to note the unevenness of change. The new technology has not completely overtaken the shopfloor as workers provided evidence of reliance on traditional skills and human performance. The shift toward post-Fordism is not automatic, nor is it linear. Rather, it is nested and contingent upon a multitude of factors, including available resources, market demand, and labor supply.

The context in which the labor process is embedded is largely defined by the global economy. Several processes of social change are active at this level. Globalization entails the potential for outsourcing, international marketing, and tight labor markets. Restructuring and spatialization underlie shifts toward just-in-time and quick-respond methods. As a result, work relations at the local level are laden with contradictions. On the one hand, workers are required to acquire skills for new machinery. On the other hand, these new skills limit traditional discretion and replace workers' control over quality with technology. In many cases, the new skills remove any possibility of workers producing beyond the pre-determined rate.

To conclude, the remaking of the labor process has both advantaged and disadvantaged workers on the shopfloor in Fieldcrest Cannon mills. However, as presented in the chapter on community impacts, the consequences of global social change occur unevenly and through a complex web of embedded social relationships. As will be discussed in the final chapter of this book, the local effects should not be surprising given the current economic context, namely global competition.

Chapter Eight

Contextualizing Change in a Southern Mill Village

Large-scale change, such as the growth of a community, usually comes slowly and unannounced. In Kannapolis, remnants of a textile village remain. The uniform, mostly white-painted mill houses, the mill factory on a hill surrounded by the town, the company name on schools, recreation centers, the library, and the name of the new minor league baseball team ("Boilweavers") reflect a heritage of textile dominance. However, Kannapolis has not escaped modernization. Regional economic development has brought hotels, shopping centers, and large retail outlets. The urban sprawl of Charlotte creeps into the mill village and redefines the labor market area. New housing developments can also be seen, as can new residents. Hispanics have opened restaurants and ethnic specialty stores. Change has come to Kannapolis, and the town is experiencing the problems that characterize other localities in the 1990s—low wages, plant closings, and racial tensions. These problems are embedded in processes of globalization, restructuring, and spatialization. It is this link between local and global that is most difficult to recognize, and even harder to make dynamic. Typically, the social context goes unnoticed in the day-to-day lives of residents. If allowed to remain unquestioned, the conditions become resistant to change as individuals deny their own agency.

The current period of rapid economic growth, including social and demographic changes that perpetuate inequalities, reflects the need to understand local and global processes as connected to one another. The central concern of my research is to understand how global restructuring is shaping the transformation of communities. As presented in Chapter Three, this concern makes it imperative that researchers critically examine existing notions of globalization and the manner in which we conceptualize and study global-local linkages. One particular concern with the globalization literature has been its tendency to treat global and local as dichotomous rather than relational constructs. Another concern is the

tendency to treat globalization as a phenomenon limited solely as something that happens overseas. Such conceptualizations result in structural
models that place global actors (TNCs, GATT, NAFTA) as determinants of
social change. Such a categorization minimizes local histories, ignores
diversity of social agents and their relative power, while downplaying con-
tinuities, and over-emphasizes fractures such as the Fordist/post-Fordist
dichotomy.

Some United States firms, such as Fieldcrest Cannon, have not been pro-
active in pursuing non-United States markets, suppliers, or overseas expansion. However, we should not take this to mean that globalization is
without influence on these firms. Quite the contrary is true. Globalization
is not defined solely on the existence of foreign markets and international
trade. In accordance with the theoretical ideas of embeddedness and social
relations, the significance of globalization for this particular case is evident
when researchers focus on the *process* of globalization rather than the *outcome.*

The United States textile-mill complex is embedded in the global economy. As Chapter Three illustrates, worldwide textile competition has
strengthened and potential markets (suppliers and retailers) are international. Changes in the world economy since World War II, including the
development project and the globalization project, directly affect the textile-mill complex. Firms in the United States textile-mill complex no longer
dominate end markets, control production, or regulate supply. The international balance between supply and demand shifts as new firms and countries enter the global market.

Globalization is part of the context of textile production and marketing
and is relevant because the entire textile-mill complex is involved in an
international economic market. The embeddedness of United States firms
in the globalization project subjects them to international forces, regardless
of demonstrations of agency. If researchers were to focus on globalization
as a dichotomous outcome, then we would miss its covert influences.
However, by conceptualizing it as a process, we can conclude that globalization does influence firms in the United States textile-mill complex.

The process of economic restructuring has similar consequences when
viewed uncritically. Like the fluidity of globalization, restructuring by capitalists to overcome local or regional limits to accumulation does not occur
in neat, concrete stages. Rather, the process spreads unevenly and can be
very heterogeneous. As shown in Chapter Four, the 1970s and 1980s were
critical transition years for the United States textile-mill complex, with the
rise of international competition and new technology. Textile firms have
responded with shifts toward consumer/retailer driven production, automated machinery, advanced technology, corporate mergers, growth in the
share of foreign owned or controlled companies, decline in the number of
textile firms, decreases in employment, and new divisions of labor. In this

study, family ownership, entrepreneurial ownership, and corporate merger have restructured the firm itself. With these changes came new workplace rules (i.e., the decline of paternalism), innovative technologies (i.e., shuttleless looms and continuous processing), and transformed production structures (i.e., team work, JIT, and QR). However, shopfloor conversion has not occurred uniformly; rather, management has introduced bits and pieces of new technology over time, necessitating the continual use of old machinery and techniques.

The process of spatialization encapsulates the unevenness of social change. The use of spatial relocation (or threats) will continue to serve as an important strategy for controlling labor. State policies often provide incentives for firms to relocate or build new manufacturing facilities. On the national level, policies such as NAFTA and GATT support industry-wide production for specific countries. On a local level, individual states offer tax breaks to lure firms. Moreover, with increased mobility of labor, management can rely on workers from other countries to increase the supply of cheap labor. Facilitated by advanced communication and transportation systems, spatialization allows employers to geographically move capital, avoiding high labor costs. At times, this may mean corporate flight, global expansion, or outsourcing. But sometimes, as was the case with Fieldcrest Cannon, the "global" comes to the local in the form of immigrant workers.

Chapter Five demonstrates the specific impacts of the processes of spatialization (as well as restructuring and globalization) for Fieldcrest Cannon. The unevenness of change and variation was evident in the three historical phases of company history. James Cannon choose to buy land near existing plants and capture local labor markets. Charles Cannon followed this pattern by not allowing incorporation of Kannapolis. After the Cannon family sold the mills, other industries moved into the area. New owner David Murdock aggressively implemented restructuring strategies and cut jobs with automation. The mill village began disintegrating, and by the time Cannon merged with Fieldcrest, the old patterns of spatial control were dissolved. More plants closed, more jobs were cut, and new industries entered the labor market to capture the surplus supply of cheap labor. This trend escalated in the 1990s as Fieldcrest Cannon incorporated new immigrant labor into its workforce.

Thus, we see that the three processes influence local communities and workplaces. Nevertheless, researchers should employ caution in interpretations. It is dangerous to focus too heavily on any one process or to single one out over the others. While analyzed independently, it is more appropriate to conceptualize globalization, spatialization, and restructuring jointly as social relations. All are historically relevant parts of modern social change. The processes co-exist in an intertwining, mutually reinforcing manner.

UNDERSTANDING GLOBAL-LOCAL: STRENGTHS AND WEAKNESSES

A key research question for this study was: how does the global impact the local? As demonstrated in this case study, processes of social change define the linkages between levels of analysis. Current key processes include globalization, restructuring, and spatialization. The processes are dynamic and have varying impacts. Each process exists in social relation to the others. Processes are embedded in a social context that is largely defined by capitalists who benefit from the power of the state.

Given the prevalence of globalization, restructuring, and spatialization in our current economic era, the multi-level model utilized for this case should be applicable to other industries and communities. One of the strengths of the current study lies in its use of a multi-level analysis, which exposes various market contingencies. Another strength is the inclusion of both workplace and community outcomes. The reconstruction of theory also proves to be an asset, as researchers can overcome theoretical weaknesses common to the frameworks of paternalism and structural-exploitation by the incorporation of embeddedness and social relations.

Obtaining data from a variety of sources was important. The demographic, historical, and qualitative findings complemented each other, increasing the validity of conclusions. Perhaps most interesting was the interviewing strategy that tapped into a variety of social locations, covering different relationships with the firm. The set of informants included social workers, company executives, textile professors, mill workers, ex-mill workers, women, men, blacks, whites, and Hispanics. The research team established good rapport with the overwhelming majority of respondents, providing lengthy and detailed interview data. Additionally, the convergence of interview data was remarkable—for the most part, all respondents told similar stories of change.

However, the informants do not constitute a random sample. The sample is biased toward older, pro-union mill workers. One possible problem with such a bias is that the informants may have tended to "romanticize" the past in their interviews. Indeed, it is difficult to judge the veracity of historical reflections. Although the informants' comments reflect particular social locations, I did not attempt to deconstruct these social locations for potential biases. The goal of interviewing was not to understand the worldviews of respondents. Rather, the goal was to understand changes in the labor market and community. I interviewed informants with the assumption that they could accurately describe such changes. Validity and reliability are supported with the triangulation of data (historical, demographic, interview) and with the consistency of description across different types of informants (university professors, textile executives, workers, community leaders, and economic developers).

Despite best intentions, weaknesses are evident in my research. When I undertook this research, I was forced to make a decision not uncommon for sociologists: do I look at a narrow topic intensively or step back and take a broad view? At the risk of missing detailed accounts of everyday life, I chose to focus on social forces creating change in the Kannapolis community. My goal was to link global forces with local outcomes. Perhaps the approach began too broadly and I sacrificed depth for breadth. Unlike conventional ethnographic studies, the qualitative data just scratch the surface. Dissimilar to quantitative studies, census data was only used for description, not regression or modeling. With time and detail, however, it should be possible to extend the project to these levels.

In addition, the problem of case generalizability remains. Is Fieldcrest Cannon idiosyncratic? Just how representative is this firm? Additionally, can we generalize from the processes identified? What are the consequences of limiting research of social forces to one firm, town, and time? These are questions most qualitative researchers face at some point. While justification for method ultimately lies in epistemological assumptions, it is imperative that the researcher acknowledges such shortcomings.

Trained social scientists can find additional limitations in the interview networks. Although the informant group was diverse (a notable strength), the number of Hispanic respondents was small, and there were no interviews with anti-union advocates. I did not undertake formal network analysis to examine the connections among respondents. According to qualitative researchers, it is often difficult to decide to leave the field. In this particular case, significant activity continues in the Kannapolis community around issues of Hispanic immigration, unionization, and economic development. Indeed, the research site continues to be a resource for exploring global-local linkages.

I acknowledge that one could address the research questions with a variety of methodological approaches. One alternative method would have been to emphasize organizational networks, focusing on networks at both community and commodity chain levels. For example, researchers can explore community networks through network analysis that links members via association with each other. Doing so may expose some of the biases inherent in the sample (i.e., respondents having common membership in a particular club) as well as connect key actors in the community. Exploring networks at the organizational level, on the other hand, might focus on the market concentration and centralization that is increasing the power of retailers. Both approaches could provide valuable insight to issues of change in southern textile villages.

Another potential criticism is that I could have given greater attention to the labor market area and less to the labor process. In particular, some might argue that the main causal factor of change for Kannapolis residents is the expansion of the Charlotte-Mecklenburg area, resulting in increased employment opportunities. The current study described this phenomenon but did not explain it. One could draw the conclusion that overall, the changes have been positive for community members. However, I urge caution in relying on simplistic explanations. As described earlier, we should avoid conceptualizing processes of social change as mutually exclusive, dichotomous, or linear. It is quite probable that the alternative interpretations reinforce and support, rather than negate each other.

In sum, multi-level, multi-method research is difficult and time consuming; researchers should remember that complex problems demand complex answers. For the community members in Kannapolis, I can offer no easy solution. Yes, global forces are influencing local circumstances in both positive and negatives ways. As agents of change, however, people have the ability to redefine their situations. For some, seeking employment in the Charlotte area provides the most opportunity. For others, remaining in the mills may be best. And for still others, learning new skills through community college courses could help. Regardless of the direction taken, it is important for people to connect their day-to-day lives with large-scale forces of change. As one respondent stated, "the most important thing workers can do is learn about what's going on around them." Knowledge of alternatives may provide access to multiple solutions, enabling community members to be more flexible during periods of change.

THEORETICAL RECONSTRUCTION

We can use the findings from this study to extend the theoretical frameworks of paternalism and structural-exploitation. As identified in Chapter One, traditional theories used to explain change in southern textiles are useful yet limited. Paternalism, which emphasizes workplace and community, focuses on localized accounts of relations between workers and company owners. By expanding the social context, structural-exploitation provides a means of interpreting processes at a system level. Merging these strengths into an alternative theory of social change can repair weaknesses, such as the cultural and market determinism, of the original frames.

In part, these strains reflect and perpetuate the division of academic study into specialized sub-areas and topics. For example, some scholars may study consequences of firm downsizing in a textile community by focusing on workers' social-psychological outcomes, such as identity and self-esteem. Others may study the same problem and limit analysis to economic indicators of income inequality. While resulting in numerous valuable independent studies, the results are not always unified across specific foci. This fragmentation leads to inadequate explanations of the mechanisms and processes of social change. For example, a paternalist frame of analysis may not include global processes of change that inevitably influence relations between workers and owners. A structural-exploitation frame may neglect the significance of localities and geographic variation that facilitate the processes of capital accumulation. Moreover, perhaps most importantly, segmented analyses deny the embeddedness of multiple levels and the strength and complexity of dynamic relationships among them.

Such limitations reflect serious obstacles to our understanding of social change, an extremely complex problem that scholars will not resolve by continued fragmentation of research into separate areas of investigation. Rather, we need a reconstructed theoretical approach conceptualizing globalization, restructuring, and spatialization as processes rather than dichotomous outcomes. Understanding processes, the mechanisms of social change, results in more than simply documenting instances of reality—it provides the tools for challenging and changing oppression (Giddens 1984; Marx 1857, 1858; Weber 1903-1917/1949).

As noted, there are two key limitations to research on textile workers, mills, and mill villages. First, researchers tend to emphasize a single process (i.e., restructuring, globalization, or spatialization) over others, thereby creating a hierarchy of those processes. For example, paternalist approaches tend to emphasize relations between workers and owners within a community, without much attention to the existence or effects of global economic change. That limitation may be a function of history—at the time when the paternalist frame developed, global forces were perhaps much less relevant than today. Structural-exploitation, on the other hand, may focus on firm restructuring at the expense of globalization and/or spatialization. No doubt, this is in part due to the emergence of structural-exploitation theory in reaction to recent United States firm economic downsizing, deindustrialization, and labor market segmentation. While both views provide insight, for the most part researchers disjoin the processes of restructuring, globalization, and spatialization, fragmenting the mechanisms that produce and reproduce inequality and denying the influence of the totality.

The second key problem with many textile studies is that the researchers magnify the micro-macro dualism or structure-agency dichotomy (see Alexander 1988; Habermas 1984). Much qualitative textile research, such as oral histories and community studies, neglects the broader social forces affecting households, including economic restructuring and globalization (e.g., Blewett 1990; Byerly 1986). In contrast, many quantitative textile studies focus primarily on structural positions and view individuals as passive objects rather than social actors (e.g., Schulman, Zingraff, Reif 1985; Wood 1986). Like mainstream sociological research on inequality (e.g., the new structuralism), statistical studies of textile workers and communities often fail to articulate the potential of human action, or agency, in the social creation, maintenance, and alteration of structures. When researchers assume structures (be they economic systems, communities, or households) *a priori*, we produce structurally determinant arguments by conceptualizing inequality as a constant, incapable of erosion (Anderson and Roscigno 1995; Anderson and Tomaskovic-Devey 1995). Additionally, few, if any, sociologists researching the issues surrounding United States textiles (both qualitative and quantitative) provide adequate attention to the impacts of global change. Finally, researchers considering processes such as restructuring often assume them self-activating or inevitable, rather than acknowledging that *people* activate such processes. Approaches that rely on market forces absolve individual, corporate, and state responsibility for change.

We can see an example of these problems in commodity-systems analyses. Although a useful heuristic device, strict adherence to the commodity chain redirects attention from processes to outcomes. That is, instead of understanding the mechanisms that create change, commodity chain researchers emphasize the contingency of effects within a "rational" market. Although such interpretation is not necessarily incorrect, the emphasis on inter-organizational networks and power shifts along the chain downplays globalization and the world economy and limits analyses to predefined market boundaries. Additionally, over-reliance on the commodity chain draws attention away from the global-local linkages that integrate community and individual with firm and industry.

To address these problems, I proposed two theoretical claims for reconstructing theories of paternalism and structural-exploitation. The first theoretical claim is *embeddedness.* To assume embeddedness is to locate individuals, groups, and structures in social and spatial contexts. For example, individuals within a specific historical context construct economic structures, such as markets (Granovetter 1992; Mingione 1991). As such, any type of economic analysis must extend beyond the market. Consequentially, researchers must analyze work activities in the context of an overall household survival strategy, or the social reproduction of the household. Mingione (1991) provides one way to visualize this—work activities (such as paid employment) are embedded in households (which support, nurture and reproduce workers), which are, in turn, embedded in other networks (kinships, religious, etc.) and structures of redistribution (grocery stores, commerce, etc.). This results in a multi-layered conceptualization of the embeddedness of work activities, centering on the household. Members of the household organize their work activities in the context of the overall reproductive strategy. Embeddedness is complicated when we recognize that structures and available resources both facilitate and constrain the individuals who construct institutions (Granovetter 1992). Thus, any resultant problematic is by definition dynamic in character.

The second theoretical claim represents an attempt to move away from static structures and categories by shifting their focus to *social relations.* By social relations, I mean the multiple processes that are historically relevant to the problem at hand. In this particular case, those processes include globalization, restructuring, and spatialization. This assumption adds movement and historical grounding to the principle of embeddedness, or the idea that individuals, groups, and structures are located in social and spatial contexts. Because of this reconceptualization, we understand structures, such as labor markets and global economies, as fluid and permeable; the experiences of individuals, while recognizably diverse, form patterned realities. The incorporation of social relations highlights the patterns of individual action that create, maintain, and change social systems. They are the mechanisms that reproduce domination and subordination, advantage and disadvantage.

Coalescing the ideas of embeddedness and social relations into an analysis of textile communities provides a more adequate understanding of the mechanisms that perpetuate the inequality than that provided by traditional explanations. Joining the various social processes, including globalization, restructuring, and spatialization, allows us to capture historical contingencies. By uniting these loose theoretical ends, we can weave the fragmented complexity of inequalities together in a tight, representative picture. The Kannapolis community and the firm Fieldcrest Cannon are embedded in a local labor market that is in turn embedded in a global economy. Marco-level processes are impacted by, and will impact upon, social relations of community and workplace. Embeddedness and social relations provide researchers with tools to expose linkages between global and local, emphasizing processes over outcomes.

SOCIAL IMPACTS OF PROCESSES: NEW WINNERS, NEW LOSERS

Together, processes of social change influence workplace and community. In Chapter Six, the social consequences for the Kannapolis community focused on three areas—changing labor markets, reconstituted ethnic relations, and household adaptations. Restructuring, globalization, and spatialization have redefined the labor market and the labor market area around the Fieldcrest Cannon mills. Kannapolis has been transformed from an isolated, insular community governed by paternalism to a community integrated into a complex regional network of jobs, housing, and commuting. Fewer textile jobs exist due to mergers, closings, and automation, but a greater number of job alternatives are present in the local labor market area due to the introduction of new manufacturing. Some ex-mill workers can obtain higher earnings in manufacturing jobs in Cabarrus County. Others, however, find that jobs in the immediate area paying below national averages are the alternative. Opportunities for better jobs exist in the Charlotte-Mecklenburg region for those with the ability to commute.

Poverty rates in Cabarrus County have remained stable, but inequality has increased. The racial composition of the area is changing—no longer are southern race relations limited to black-white dynamics. Many problems remain for the Kannapolis area. Community leader informants continuously cited lack of leadership and solidarity as significant drawbacks for residents. In addition, social services are inadequate to meet the needs of poor families. Schools, hospitals, and law enforcement are poorly prepared to handle the influx of Spanish-speaking immigrants. There is no public transportation in Kannapolis, in Cabarrus County, or along the urban corridor to Charlotte.

Consistent with other research (i.e., Bluestone and Harrison 1982; Harrison and Bluestone 1988; Fitchen 1991, 1995; Johnson 1990), the processes of globalization, restructuring, and spatialization have both negative and positive impacts on the community of Kannapolis and Cabarrus County. Economic inequality in the community has increased, widening the gap between haves and have-nots. Once again, we must avoid considering social consequences as dichotomous or all-inclusive outcomes. For some residents, the impacts have been positive. For many, the effects are mixed. The changing social processes may create new opportunities for some people, but the processes also bring increased unemployment, poverty, and earnings inequality for the community at large.

Processes of change in the community continue to occur unevenly, affecting individuals in various ways. Indeed, the structure of power and domination in this southern textile community has been modified. Perhaps it is ironic that the dismantling of paternalism has resulted in many negative consequences in the daily lives of community members. Ideally, the restructuring of the labor market should provide greater opportunities for workers. However, this is not necessarily the case. As seen here, the "free" market is embedded in complex social relations, including historical and modern pressures. The social consequences of change for Kannapolis are embedded in previous sets of social relations, perhaps the most significant being paternalism. In Kannapolis, emerging forms of social organization are rooted within industry, national, and global contexts.

In Chapter Seven, I discussed the social impacts specific to the workplace. Changes in firm and the structure of industry alter shopfloor labor processes; examples include increased production pace, new management strategies, and technological adjustments. The structure and culture of the shopfloor in Fieldcrest Cannon plants has been reconfigured around three areas—redefining jobs, teamwork, and unsteady employment.

At Fieldcrest Cannon, bureaucratization and increasing standardization has resulted in the deskilling of labor (Braverman 1974), but only to a partial extent. In many instances, old skills, such as those used by loom fixers, remain indispensable. At the same time, new skills such as literacy and ability to communicate are required. Management has also changed forms of worker-control. As Edwards (1979) suggests, however, each transformation does not require absolution of previous forms. From interviewing workers at Fieldcrest Cannon, it is evident that various forms of control, including paternal (simple), technical, and bureaucratic, often overlap and reinforce one another.

Millwork in Kannapolis has improved in many ways. Plants are not as dirty and dangerous as they were before the industry restructuring of the 1980s. But workers complain about stressful demands, such as increased production rates and coordination of team members, and lack of company loyalty. Management dismissed many workers as the labor process became increasingly automated. Remaining millwork is demanding. The complexity of new technology requires different skills from workers. At the same time, the upgrading serves to deskill workers. Management no longer relies on traditional forms of knowledge about textile production. Management uses technology, not worker skill, to control quality.

Bureaucratic rules have replaced traditional forms of control in textile mills (Leiter 1982). In the case of Fieldcrest Cannon, management expresses bureaucratic rules by requiring teamwork and cooperation among workers. Nevertheless, this form of control is embedded in a market economy that emphasizes profits over people. Changes in the organization of the labor market and nature of jobs, such as tight labor pools, may increase racial and skill divisions on the shopfloor and make it difficult for teams to run smoothly. This fact should reminds us that new technologies and management strategies are not neutral and ultimately serve to benefit capitalists.

At the same time, alterations in the labor process occur unevenly. Workers provided evidence of reliance on traditional skills and human performance. The new technology has not overtaken the shopfloor. The shift toward post-Fordism is not automatic, nor is it linear. Rather, it is nested and contingent upon a multitude of factors, including available resources, market demand, and labor supply.

The context in which the labor processes is embedded is largely defined by the global economy. Several processes of social change are active at this level. Globalization entails the potential for outsourcing, international marketing, and new labor markets. Restructuring and spatialization underlie retail-demanded shifts toward just-in-time and quick-respond methods of production. As a result, work relations at the local level are laden with contradictions. On the one hand, workers are required to acquire skills for new machinery. On the other hand, these new skills limit traditional discretion and replace worker's control over quality with technology. In many cases, the new skills remove any possibility of workers producing beyond the pre-determined rate.

AGENCY: ALTERING SOCIAL RELATIONS

Although not a focus of this study, we cannot ignore the potential for unionization among Fieldcrest Cannon workers. Numerous respondents referenced previous union struggles as well as the possibility of a future drive. In terms of "voting in the union," Kannapolis members of ACTWU have been unsuccessful. However, when we shift focus away from the outcome to the process, Kannapolis residents have made significant advances against tremendous obstacles. As the community history suggests, these mill workers are not passive recipients of repression. Paternalism, while influential, has not removed agency from community members. However, other forces are at work to control labor. For example, evidence shows that the state of North Carolina has stepped in to suppress strikes. Less obvious are firm-based incentives provided by the state, such as tax breaks, that lure companies to areas of high unemployment. Textile workers seeking unionization must battle more than the company. The uprising of textile workers will always be embedded in a context of firm, community, state, and national control of labor. Successful outcomes require negotiation of multiple levels. Nevertheless, with each step in the struggle, the critical awareness of some workers increases, opening the potential for alternative forms of insurgency.

We find one such alternative attempt to gain power over the firm and state in the organization efforts of Piedmont Peace Project (PPP), a local grassroots agency based on community rather than workplace. During fieldwork, I had a three-hour interview with an organizer for PPP, covering her life history in textile work as well as details of the organization. Members of PPP include low-income residents of rural North Carolina communities of all races—African-American, Native American, Hispanic, Laotian, and white. Members include farmers, textile-mill workers, retirees, domestic workers, truck drivers, parents, and young people. According to the group's brochure, "we use common sense organizing to empower disenfranchised, low-income folks through our work in literacy, community organizing, voter registration and education, and youth organizing." PPP has organized non-partisan voter registration, offered leadership programs that "help poor people learn to use their voices and their government to help themselves," as well as training programs aimed at teaching wealthy people to work with the poor.

PPP's approach to social change is from the bottom up, allowing community residents to define important issues. Utilizing block grants, PPP provides the technical resources and training so that communities such as Kannapolis can speak out for themselves and determine the types of services they need. Often the goal has been as simple as getting community dumpsters or stop signs in low income, rural communities.

One of the benefits of PPP's approach is the focus on issues (i.e., voter registration) rather than identities (i.e., textile worker, woman, black). This approach tends to unite and solidify members—including those of different races and social class—a key resource in an area where capitalists have a successfully history of "divide and conquer" labor strategy. Why did PPP emerge with a focus on issues? Perhaps its creation is due to the decline in number of textile jobs, increases in heterogeneity of workforce, and past problems resulting in unsuccessful unionization. When examined in terms of embeddedness, PPP emerged in the context of changes in the organization and structure of work and the history of unionization.

When seeking to understand group struggle, it is crucial to recognize the interactive nature of subordination processes and the embeddedness of such processes in social organization. As stated earlier, social relations are not simply outcomes. Rather, they are processes that researchers must view as both organizing principles of social identity and organizing principles of social structure. The fact that processes become deep-seated, institutionalized, and routine in organizational structures suggests a need for identification of practices that exist at multiple levels (e.g., the family, the workplace, religion, education, the local economy, the state, etc.) and that currently perpetuate inequalities. One way to bridge these levels, as PPP is attempting to do, is with a focus on issues that unite various groups of people.

At this time, I cannot predict the extent to which groups such as ACTWU or PPP will alter social relations in Kannapolis. Influential elements include effective leadership, resources, timing, persistence, and the embeddedness of inequality. Central as well are beliefs, goals, and strategies that recognize enduring processes and complex structures of inequality and that attempt to rectify them, thereby moving us toward a more just society. Efforts of insurgent individuals and groups help make the linkages between global change and local outcomes visible, increasing the potential for agency and the alteration of existing social relations.

Afterword

After the union defeat of 1993, in which the union lost by 199 votes out of more than 6,000 ballots cast, workers charged the company with using unfair tactics. Specific complaints included registering and voting in the names of deceased people, posting threats of deportation in Spanish, and drawing artificial lines to keep union organizers away from the plant. The workers' claims proved valid. In 1995, after years of litigation, the National Labor Relations Board (NLRB) charged Fieldcrest Cannon with unfair labor practices. Among other things, the NLRB found the company guilty of intimidation, coercion, and harassment of employees (*Raleigh News and Observer*, September 6, 1995). The NLRB rejected an appeal of the decision by Fieldcrest Cannon, and a new election was held in August 1997. As in 1991, the union was defeated in 1997, this time by 369 votes out of the 4,757 votes counted (*Raleigh News and Observer*, August 14, 1997).

Shortly after the 1997 union defeat, Pillowtex, a Texas-based manufacturer of high-end home furnishings, announced that it was acquiring Fieldcrest Cannon to create the third largest U.S. home furnishings textile company (*Charlotte Observer*, September 12, 1997). While Fieldcrest Cannon became a subsidiary of Dallas-based Pillowtex, the newly merged firm made a commitment to maintaining a significant operating presence in Kannapolis. Chuck Hansen Jr., CEO of Pillowtex stated that the name on the Kannapolis plants would not change: "We're not going to put Pillowtex up there . . . Cannon has so much heritage. That would be an insult to Kannapolis and North Carolina" (The *Durham Herald-Sun*, February 9, 1998: B6).

The series of mergers, combined with industry-wide restructuring and local labor market expansion, furthered the deterioration of paternalist social capital. The merger with Pillowtex was announced only one month after the failed 1997 vote and while a complaint filed by UNITE accusing

Fieldcrest management of unfair tactics and violating federal court orders and labor laws was pending with the National Labor Relations Board. UNITE began a new union organizing drive coincident with the merger focusing on increased work demands, job changes, pension benefits, and job security. According to Bruce Raynor, the union's organizing director, Pillowtex management opposed the union, but obeyed the labor laws and did not resort to threats. In June 1999, workers voted 2,270 to 2,102 for the union in an election described as the cleanest ever (*The New York Times*, June 25, 1999). Pillowtex accepted the union victory and began negotiations in November 1999, resulting in a contract covering 5,000 workers in the plants around Kannapolis and 3,500 workers in other Fieldcrest plants. Workers won modest increases in wages, paid sick days, and pension benefits. UNITE promised to work with the financially troubled Pillowtex to ensure that the plants remain competitive by having productive and motivated workers who have a stake in the future of the company.

Semi-Structured Interview Guides

Kannapolis / June 1995

Introduction of self and explanation of purpose of research.

Hi. My name is Cindy Anderson. I'm a researcher at North Carolina State University. I'm involved in a study on changes in North Carolina textile communities. I've read a lot about the history of your community and its major industry. Recently, there has been a lot of change in textile communities. Many local firms have been sold or have merged with other companies. There's been a lot of competition coming from non-US companies. Such changes filter down to the workers, and affect them and their families. What I want to know is how the people of your community are adjusting to these changes. What kinds of things are going on in the lives of people like you?

So that's what I want to talk about today. I have a few questions to guide our discussion, but I'm mostly interested in your ideas and opinions about what's going on. Any experiences you wish to share will help me construct a picture of how changes in the textile industry are affecting people in the community. I want to assure you that what you say will be confidential and anonymous—your name will not appear in any report, nor will what you say be used to identify you.

First, I have an "informed consent" letter that I'd like you to sign. This means that you are willingly entering the discussion, and that you understand the nature of the interview. It also says that we guarantee our conversation to be confidential and your identity will remain anonymous. University rules require that we get your signature before we start. Please take your time looking it over.

1. Background

Ok, just to get started—would you tell me a little about yourself?

Probe for age, education, gender, race, how long in Kannapolis.

If respondent seems to be at ease, then continue with personal information about work status (2) and family background (3); if respondent is ill at ease, then switch to local economy questions (4) and return to work status and family background later in the interview.

2. Work Status

Next, I would like to know about your work...

What do you (did you) do to make a living?

For whom do you work?

How long have you worked at this place?

Do you now or have you ever had other types of jobs?

Probe for

–multiple job holding

–breaks in employment/unemployment

–full time/part-time work

Have you ever worked in a textile mill? Have any members of your family ever worked in a mill?

Probe for
– textile mill jobs and relationship to Cannon Mills

– If non-mill worker, go on to next section (4) on local economy.

– If current / former mill worker, probe for questions about how work has changed.

How has work in the mills changed? EXAMPLE

Do different types of people work for Cannon today? LIKE WHO?

Have the jobs people hold changed? EXAMPLE

What about the machines in the mill—have they changed since you started working?

What about management—has it changed?

What about the hours and types of work that people do?

Probe for changes in technology, labor process, and shift work.

3. Family

Tell me about your family history...

Did you grow up in Kannapolis?

Where were your grandparents from? What did they do?

Where were your parents from? What did they do?

Any brothers or sisters? What do they do?

Probe for family involvement in mills.

How many people live with you?

Tell me about them—what do they do, how old are they, how are they related to you?

4. Local Economy

Ok—the next set of topics is on changes in the local economy. I said earlier that we're interested in studying the impact of economic changes.

Tell me what it means to you when I say there have been major changes in the local economy.

Probe: What major changes have occurred in your community's economy (i.e., business & industry) in the last 10 years?

Have businesses closed?

What has grown?

Do you think this is for the better or worse?

Do people commute to other areas? (Charlotte, LMA). Where?

What do they do there?

How have all these changes affected you?

Has is affected your work?

What about your responsibilities around home?

Why do you think these changes are happening?

What can you do about it?

Who in this community has been most helped by the changes? Most hurt?

Probe: What types of people... groups...

5. Survival Strategies & Networks

Overall, have things gotten better or worse for folks over the last few years?

What do people do when they fall upon hard times?

If somebody lost their job, where would they go for help?

Note: pay careful attention to how subject responds. If they seem OK, could follow with personal questions; e.g., has this ever happened to you?

If someone was unemployed, how would he/she find a new job?

Where would somebody go for help?

Where would they go to get another job?

Are there any re-training programs in the community?

Are there any services to help people who don't have work?

What types of people use these services?

Do folks help each other out during hard times? How so?

Besides work, do people do other things to help them get by?

Do they share things with each other or swap things?

Probe for bartering, non-cash work, networking, exchanging, self-provisioning, etc.

Probe for government programs...

What about public programs?

Does the city or state of NC seem to help?

6. Community

What do folks do around here outside of work and home?

Probe: clubs, YMCA, church, recreation...

7. Mobilization

From reading the paper, there seemed to be a lot of conflict around the mills in Kannapolis during the 1980s.

Could you tell me about what you think about what went on?

What made some people go out and participate? Did you know people involved?

Probe for information about the unionization struggle. Who joined? Who opposed?

Today, if workers like you were to have a serious problem, do you think they would organize to get what they wanted?

Probe to find out what unites and divides people.

8. Gender

Now, I want to know about the different types of people in your community. I am especially interested in how people get along together.

Let's talk about men and women.

How do men and women get along at work? Tensions? Work in same jobs?

Is being a man or a women important for the types of jobs people have?

What types of jobs do women have? Men?

Probe specifically for information about textile work.

What are the household responsibilities of women? Of men?

Do women work while the kids are growing up?

Who takes care of them when they get sick or hurt?

How do household members help out with things?

Probe for work and home involvement.

Do you think these patterns are common for most men and women around here?

Probe for differences by class, race, etc.

How do you see the situation for women in the next 10 years? For men?

Probe: at work, at home, in community

9. Race

What about race? Many communities around the state and across the nation are experiencing racial tensions.

Is any of that going on here?

What different racial and ethnic groups do you see around here?

How do folks of different races get along?

When do different races interact?

Are men of different races likely to hang together?

How about women?

Probe for interactions of gender, race, and class.

How important is race for the types of jobs that people have?

Is there tension between racial groups in workplaces?

Probe specifically for textile work.

How do you see the situation for races in the next ten years?

Probe specifically for groups identified.

10. Overall Assessment

Ok. Just a few more questions.

All things considered, what do you think of Kannapolis as a place to live?

What do you think is the best thing about Kannapolis?

What do you think is the worst thing about Kannapolis?

If you had the power to change one thing about Kannapolis, what would you change?

Overall, how do you think things will change in the next ten years? Better or worse?

11. Conclusion of Interview

Well, that wraps up my questions. We covered a lot of ground, and your comments were very helpful. Are there any concerns you'd like to add?

Maybe issues I didn't raise?

Thanks for your time and cooperation; we really appreciate your help in our research.

Before we leave, do you know of other people who might be interested in talking with us?

Let me give you my card; please call if anything else comes up.

INTERVIEW GUIDE FOR HISPANIC CONNECTIONS

Hi. My name is Cindy Anderson. I am a researcher in the sociology department at North Carolina State University. I'm currently involved with a project examining changes in labor markets in North Carolina, such as the Charlotte-Mecklenburg area. One thing we've noticed is the significant growth of Hispanic workers. Your name was provided to us by someone at Central Piedmont Community College as a person who is knowledgeable about the Hispanic community in the Charlotte-Mecklenburg area. We are especially interested in the entry of Hispanics into industrial and manufacturing jobs. Would you have some time to talk with me about general issues related to these topics?

It will only take 10 or 15 minutes.
I can talk now, or call back at a more convenient time...

Before we begin, let me assure you that our conversation will be confidential. I am only interested in you as an informant, as someone knowledgeable about the community. OK?

First, tell me about your relationship with Hispanic communities in North Carolina (i.e., Who are you and what do you do? How long have you been in area?).

Newspapers have reported tremendous growth in numbers of Hispanics coming to the area. Do you agree with this?

Where are they coming from? (Probe—Central America? Mexico?)

Who is coming? Entire families? Men only?

Where do they live and work?

What kinds of jobs are they getting? (Probe for manufacturing and industry jobs.)

Are they getting training and assistance from state or local agencies?

How have other workers (i.e., long-time residents) reacted?

What are some of the biggest problems facing Hispanic workers?

*If person seems to have "experiential knowledge," ask if we can follow up our discussion with a visit and have them show us around. (i.e., "We'll be making future visits to your area. Would you be willing to meet with us?")

Sample Letters of Inquiry

Dear Community Resident:

We are seeking your participation in a research study about the impacts of economic change in your community. The textile industry has changed dramatically in recent decades. No doubt your lives have been affected in some way. Our purpose is to better understand those impacts as a first step toward formulating community development policy.

The study has three parts. We are looking at the history of your community and its major businesses, the current socioeconomic conditions of your community and its residents, and the views of people like you. We would like your participation in an interview. We will ask questions about your work and family history, including job and family responsibilities. The interview will take place in a local center or home and last approximately one hour.

It is important to know that names will not be used in our study. We are interested only in "what" people have experienced, not "who" says what. Your signature on the next page shows your voluntary permission to be interviewed. All information collected is confidential, and your name will not be used in any part of the study.

The study is funded by a research grant from the United States Department of Agriculture. Dr. Michael Schulman, a professor at North Carolina State University, is coordinating this project. The research associate for this project is Cindy Anderson, a Ph.D. student at North Carolina State University. Interviews will be done by both researchers. Upon completion, the results from this study will be used to guide policy makers concerned with improving the lives of rural community members.

We appreciate your participation in this study. We believe this study is important to the lives of individuals in your community and those in similar circumstances. Thank you for your time and energy.

Sincerely,

Cindy Anderson

Dear Community Leader:

We are seeking your participation in a research study about the impacts of economic change in local labor markets. Kannapolis, Cabarrus County, and the surrounding areas represent one of the our research sites. In particular, we are interested in changes in industry and job growth and decline. The study has three parts. We are looking at the history of the community, the current socioeconomic conditions of the community and its residents, and the interpretations and experiences of people living in the community. As such, we would like your participation in an interview. We will ask questions about the local economy, including industry and employment. If convenient, the interview will take place in your office and last approximately one hour.

The study is funded by a research grant from the United States Department of Agriculture. Dr. Michael Schulman, a professor at North Carolina State University, is coordinating this project. The research associate for this project is Cindy Anderson, a Ph.D. student at North Carolina State University. Interviews will be done by both researchers. Upon completion, the results from this study will be used to guide policy makers concerned with changes facing many North Carolina communities. All information collected is confidential, and your name will not be used in any part of the study. Your signature on the next page shows your voluntary permission to be interviewed.

We appreciate your participation in this study. We believe this study is important to the community, to the lives of individuals in your community, and to those in similar circumstances. Thank you for your time and energy.

Sincerely,

Cindy Anderson

List of Field Visits and Interviews

Notes.000	NCSU textile professor
Notes.001	Preliminary Interview Group
Notes.002	Dec. 6-7, 1994: visit with retired white male textile worker
	Tour Kannapolis including the Visitor's Center
Notes.003	June 13, 1995: Piedmont Peace Project
	Meeting with one retired white male textile worker and one white male terminated textile worker.
Interv.001	white couple; female textile worker, male terminated textile worker
Interv.002	white male disabled textile worker
Interv.003	white female textile worker
Interv.004	white male, economic developer
Interv.005	white male, economic developer
Interv.006	black male, minister
Interv.007	white female, social service worker
Interv.008	black female, retired domestic workers
Interv.009	black male, ex-textile worker
Interv.010	black male/female couple, both textile workers
Interv.011	white male/female couple, male retired textile worker
Interv.012	black female, community activist (taped interview)
Interv.013	white female, textile worker
Interv.014	white male, retired textile worker
Interv.015	white male, county extension agent
Interv.016	white male, retired labor organizer
Interv.017	white female, lawyer
Interv.018	white female, textile worker
Interv.019	white male, textile worker
Interv.020	NCSU textile professor

Interv.021	NCSU textile professor
Interv.022	Executive Vice President, Fieldcrest Cannon
Interv.023	Tour of Fieldcrest Cannon plant and interviews with two managers (one white male and one white female)
Interv.024	Hispanic couple, community leaders
Interv.025	Phone interview with white male terminated textile worker (follow-up)
Notes.031	Notes from graduate seminar in textiles, NCSU

Bibliography

Agar, M.H. 1986. *Speaking of ethnography*. Beverly Hills: Sage Pub.

Aggarwal, V. 1985. *Liberal protectionism: The international politics of organized textile trade*. Berkeley, CA: University of California Press.

Alexander, J.C. 1988. *Action and its environments: Toward a new synthesis*. NY: Columbia University Press.

Amin, A. and N. Thrift. 1994. "Living in the global." Pp. 1–22 in *Globalization, institutions and regional development in Europe*, edited by A. Amin and N. Thrift. NY: Oxford University Press.

Andersen M. L. and P.H. Collins. 1992. *Race, class, and gender: An anthology*. Belmont, CA: Wadsworth.

Anderson, C.D. 1996. "Understanding the inequality problematic: From scholarly rhetoric to theoretical reconstruction." *Gender & Society*, 10(6):729–746.

Anderson, C. D. and V. Roscigno. 1995. "Letter to the Editor: Inequality processes, solutions, and methodological approaches." *Gender & Society* 9:640–42.

Anderson, C.D. and D. Tomaskovic-Devey. 1995. "Patriarchal pressures: An exploration of organizational processes that exacerbate and erode gender earnings inequality." *Work and Occupations*, 22(3):328–356.

Anderson, C.D. and M.D. Schulman. 1999. "Women, restructuring, and textiles: The increasing complexity of subordination and struggle in a southern community." PP. 91–108 in *Neither separate nor equal: Women, race, and class in the South*, edited by B.E. Smith. Philadelphia, PA: Temple University Press.

Angel, D. 1994. *Restructuring for innovation: The remaking of the US semiconductor industry*. NY: Guilford Press.

Applebaum, R.P., D. Smith and B. Christenson. 1994. "Commodity chains and industrial restructuring in the Pacific Rim: Garment trade and manufacturing." Pp. 187–204 in *Commodity Chains: Global Capitalism*, edited by G. Gereffi and M. Korzeniewicz. Westport, CT: Greenwood Press.

Atkinson, P. and M. Hamersley. 1994. "Ethnography and participant observation." Pp. 248–261 in *Handbook of qualitative research*, edited by N.K. Denzin and Y.S. Lincoln. Thousand Oaks, CA: Sage.

Barkin, D. 1982. "The impact of agribusiness on rural development." *Current Perspectives in Social Theory* 3:1-25

Bartley, N. 1983. *The Creation of modern Georgia*. Athens, GA: University of Georgia Press.

Beatty, B. 1994. "Gender relations in Southern textiles." Pp. 9–16 In *Race, class and community in Southern labor history,* edited by G.M. Fink and M.E. Reed. Tuscaloosa: University of Alabama Press.

Beneria, L. and M. Roldan. 1987. *The crossroads of class and gender: Industrial homework, subcontracting, and household dynamics in Mexico City*. Chicago: University of Chicago Press.

Billings, D.B., Jr. 1979. *Planters and the making of a "New South": Class, politics, and development in North Carolina, 1865–1900*. Chapel Hill: University of North Carolina Press.

———— 1982. "Class origins of the 'New South': Planter persistence and industry in North Carolina." *American Journal of Sociology* 88:552–585.

———— 1990. "Religion as opposition: A Gramscian analysis." *American Journal of Sociology* 96(1):1–13.

Billings, D.B., Jr., and K.M. Blee. 1986. "Bringing history back in: The historicity of social relation." Pp. 51–68 in *Current perspectives in social theory*, volume 7, edited by J. Wilson and S.G. McNall. Greenwich, Conn.: JAI Press.

Blauner, R. 1964. *Alienation and freedom: The factory worker and his industry*. Chicago: University of Chicago Press.

Blewett, M.H., Editor. 1990. *The Last generation: Work and life in the textile mills of Lowell, Massachusetts, 1910–1960*. Amherst, MA: University of Massachusetts Press.

Bluestone, B. and B. Harrison. 1982. *The deindustrialization of America: Plant closings, community abandonment, and the dismantling of basic industry*. NY: Basic Books.

Bonacich, E. and D.V. Waller. 1994. "Mapping a global industry: Apparel production in the Pacific Rim triangle." Pp. 21–41 in *Global production: The apparel industry in the Pacific Rim*, edited by E. Bonacich, L. Cheng, N. Chinchilla, N. Hamilton, and P. Ong. Philadelphia: Temple University Press.

Bonanno, A. 1994. "The locus of policy action in a global setting." Pp. 251–264 in *From Columbus to ConAgra: The globalization of agriculture and food*, edited by A. Bonanno, L. Busch, W. Friedland, L. Gouveia, and E. Mingione. Lawrence, KS: University Press of Kansas.

Bonham, J.C. 1991. "Robotics, electronics, and the American textile industry." Pp. 163–180 in *Hanging by a thread: Social change in Southern textiles*, edited by J. Leiter, M.D. Schulman, and R. Zingraff. Ithaca, NY: ILR Press.

Borman, K.M., M.D. LeCompte and J.P. Goetz. 1986. "Ethnographic and qualitative research design and why it doesn't work." *American Behavioral Scientist,* 30(1):42–57.

Braverman, H. 1974. *Labor and monopoly capital: the degradation of work in the twentieth century.* NY: Monthly Review Press.

Burawoy, M. 1979. *Manufacturing consent: Changes in the labor process under monopoly capitalism.* Chicago: University of Chicago Press.

——— 1991. *Ethnography unbound: Power and resistance in the modern metropolis.* CA: University of CA Press.

Busch, L. 1994. "The state of agricultural science and the agricultural science of the state." Pp. 69–84 in *From Columbus to ConAgra: The globalization of agriculture and food,* edited by A. Bonanno, L. Busch, W. Friedland, L. Gouveia, and E. Mingione. Lawrence, KS: University Press of Kansas.

Buttel, F. and D. Goodman. 1989. "Class, state, technology, and international food regimes." *Sociologia Ruralis* 14(2):86–93.

Byerly, V. 1986. *Hard times cotton mill girls: Personal histories of womanhood and poverty in the South.* Ithaca, NY: ILR Press.

Carlton, D. 1982. *Mill and town in South Carolina, 1880–1920.* Baton Rouge, LA: Louisiana State University Press.

——— 1994. "Paternalism and Southern textile labor: A historiographical review." Pp. 17–26 in *Race, class and community in Southern labor history,* edited by G.M. Fink and M.E. Reed. Tuscaloosa, AL: University of Alabama Press.

Cash, W.J. 1941. *The mind of the South.* NY: Knopf.

Castells, M. 1985. "High technology, economic restructuring, and the urban regional procession in the US." Pp. 1–40 in *High technology, space and society,* edited by M. Castells. Beverly Hills, CA: Sage Publications.

Castells, M. and J. Henderson. 1987. "Techno-economic restructuring, socio-political processes and spatial transformation: A global perspective." Pp. 1–17 in *Global restructuring and territorial development,* edited by J. Henderson and M. Castells. Newbury Park, CA: Sage Pub., Inc.

Charlotte Observer. September 29, 1985. "Cannon union vote likely to echo throughout textiles."

Charlotte Observer. September 24, 1995.

Charlotte Observer. September 12, 1997. "Pillowtex to buy Fieldcrest."

Cheng, L. and G. Gereffi. 1994. "US retailers and Asian garment production." Pp. 63–79 in *Global production: The apparel industry in the Pacific Rim,* edited by E. Bonacich, L. Cheng, N. Chinchilla, N. Hamilton, and P. Ong. Philadelphia, PA: Temple University Press.

Clairmonte, F. and J. Cavanagh. 1981. *The world in their web: The dynamics of textile multinationals.* London: Zed Press.

Clawson, D. 1980. *Bureaucracy and the labor process: The transformation of US industry, 1860–1920.* NY: Monthly Review Press.

Cline, W.R. 1987. *The future of world trade in textiles and apparel.* Washington, DC: Institute for International Economics.

Collins, C.L. 1994. "Fieldcrest Cannon." Pp. 213–217 in *International directory of company histories.* Volume 9, edited by P. Kepos. Detroit, MI: St. James Press.

Collins, P.H. 1990. *Black feminist thought: Knowledge, consciousness, and politics of empowerment.* NY: Allen & Unwin.

Conway, M. 1979. *Rise gonna rise: A portrait of Southern textile workers.* Garden City, NY: Anchor Press/Doubleday.

Danziger, S. and P. Gottschalk. 1995. *America unequal.* NY: Russell Sage Foundation.

Denzin, N.K. 1989. *The research act,* (3rd edition). Englewood Cliffs, NJ: Prentice-Hall.

Dickerson, K.G. 1995. *Textiles and apparel in the global economy.* Englewood Cliffs, NJ: Prentice-Hall, Inc.

DiPrete, T.A. 1990. "Adding covariates to loglinear models for the study of social mobility." *American Sociological Review* 55(5):757–773.

DiPrete, T. and D.B. Grusky. 1990. "Structure and trend in the process of stratification for American men and women." *American Journal of Sociology* 96:107–143.

Douglas, J.D. 1985. *Creative interviewing.* Beverly Hills, CA: Sage Pub.

Durham Herald-Sun, February 9, 1998. "Businessman has big plans for Fieldcrest Cannon."

Edwards, R.C. 1979. *Contested terrain: The transformation of the workplace in the twentieth century.* NY: Basic Books.

Economic Intelligence Unit. 1992. "Special Report #2632." London: Business International Limited.

Edwards, R. 1979. *Contested terrain: The transformation of the workplace in the twentieth century.* NY: Basic Books.

Ely and Larkin 1987. *Cannon Mills Company 1887–1987: A century of progress.* Kannapolis, NC: Fieldcrest Cannon, Inc.

Emerson, R.M. 1981. "Observational field work." *The Annual Review of Sociology,* 7:351–78.

——— 1983. *Contemporary field research: A collection of readings.* Boston, MA: Little Brown & Co.

Entwisle, B. and W.M. Mason. 1985. "Multilevel effects of socioeconomic development and family planning programs on children ever born." *American Journal of Sociology.* 91:616–49.

Erlandson, D.A., E.L. Harts, B.L. Skipper, and S.D. Allen. 1993. *Doing naturalist inquiry: A guide to methods.* Newbury Park, CA: Sage Publications.

Escott, P.D. 1985. *Many excellent people: Power and privilege in North Carolina, 1850 – 1900.* Chapel Hill, NC: University of North Carolina Press.

Fieldcrest Cannon Today. October 1994.

Fink, G.M. and M.E. Reed. 1994. *Race, class, and community in Southern labor history.* Tuscaloosa, AL: The University of Alabama Press.

Finnie, T.A. 1990. "Mergermania in US textiles and clothing." Pp. 64–108 in *Economic Intelligence Unit.* London: Business International Limited.

Fitchen, J.M. 1991. *Endangered spaces, enduring places: Change, identity, and survival in rural America.* Boulder, CO: Westview Press.

——— 1994. "Residential mobility among the rural poor." *Rural Sociology* 59: 416–36.

—— 1995. "Spatial redistribution of poverty through migration of poor people to depressed rural communities." *Rural Sociology* 60(2):181–201.

Fontana, A. and J.H. Frey. 1994. "Interviewing: The art of science." Pp. 361–376 in *The handbook of qualitative research*, edited by N.K. Denzin and Y.S. Lincoln. Thousand Oaks, CA: Sage Publications.

Ford, J. 1986. "World trade in textiles." *Textiles*, 15(3):72–77.

Fothergill, S. and G. Gudgin. 1985. "Ideology and methods in industrial location research." Pp. 93–115 in *Politics and method: Contrasting studies in industrial geography*, edited by D. Massey and R. Meegan. London: Methuen.

Fox-Genovesse, E. 1988. *Within the plantation household: Black and white women of the old south*. Chapel Hill: University of North Carolina Press.

Frankel, L. 1984. "Southern textile women: Generations of survival and struggle." Pp. 39–60 in *My troubles are going to have trouble with me: Everyday trials and triumphs of women workers*, edited by K.B. Sacks and D. Remy. New Brunswick, NJ: Rutgers University Press.

Frederickson, M. 1982. "Four decades of change: workers in southern textiles, 1941–1981." *Radical America* 16(Nov.–Dec.):27–44.

—— *Sisterhood and solidarity: workers' education for women, 1914–1984*. Philadelphia, PA: Temple University Press.

Freeze, G.R. 1991. "Poor girls who might otherwise be wretched: The origins of paternalism in North Carolina's mills, 1836–1880." Pp. 21–32 in *Hanging by a thread: social change in southern textiles*, edited by J. Leiter, M. Schulman, and R. Zingraff. Ithaca, NY: ILR Press.

—— 1994. "Patriarchy lost: The precondition for paternalism in the Odell cotton mills of North Carolina, 1882–1900." Pp. 27–40 in *Race, class and community in southern labor history*, edited by G.M. Fink and M.E. Reed. Tuscaloosa, AL: University of Alabama Press.

Friedland, W., A.E. Barton, and R.J. Thomas. 1981. *Manufacturing green gold: Capital labor and technology in the lettuce industry*. NY: Cambridge University Press.

Friedland, W.H. 1984. "Commodity systems analysis: An approach to the sociology of agriculture." Pp. 221–235 in *Research in rural sociology and development*, edited by H.K. Schwarzweller. Greenwich, CT: JAI Press.

—— 1994. "The global fresh fruit and veggie system: An industrial organization analysis." Pp. 173–189 in *Global restructuring of agro–food systems*, edited by P. McMichael. Ithaca, NY: Cornell University Press.

Friedland, W.H. and D. Nellcon. 1972. "Changing perspectives in the organization of migrant farm workers in the Eastern United States." *Social Problems* 19(4):509–521.

Gans, H. 1962. *Urban villagers*. NY: Free Press.

Garrett, P. 1993. "Rural families and children in poverty." Pp. 230–58 in *Persistent poverty in rural America*, edited by G. Summers. Boulder, CA: Westview Press.

Garrett, P. and J.E. Uquillas. 1994. "Structural interviewing in Ecuador: Incorporating gender into diagnostic field research." Pp. 45–51 in *Tools for the field: Methodologies handbook for gender analysis in agriculture*, edited by H.S. Feldstein and J. Jiggirs. West Hartford, CT: Kumatian Press, Inc.

Gaventa, J. and B.E. Smith. 1991. "The deindustrialization of the textile South: A case study." Pp. 181–198 in *Hanging by a thread: Social change in southern textiles*, edited by J. Leiter, M. Schulman, and R. Zingraff. Ithaca, NY: ILR Press.

Genovesse, E.D. 1974. *Roll, Jordon, roll: The world the slaves made*. NY: Pantheon.

Gereffi, G. 1989. "Development strategies and the global factory." *Annals of Americans Academy of Political and Social Sciences* 515:92–104.

——— 1994. "The organization of buyer-driven global commodity chains: How United States retailers shape overseas production networks." Pp. 96–122 in *Commodity chains: Global capitalism*, edited by G. Gereffi and M. Korzeniewicz. Westport, CT: Greenwood Press.

Gereffi, G., M. Korzeniewicz, and R.P. Korzeniewicz. 1994. "Introduction: Global commodity chains." Pp. 1–14 in *Commodity chains: Global capitalism*, edited by G. Gereffi and M. Korzeniewicz. Westport, CT: Greenwood Press.

Giddens, A. 1984. *The constitution of society: Outline of the theory of structuration*. Berkeley: University of California Press.

Glasmeier, A.K. 1985. "Innovative manufacturing industries: Spatial incidence in the United States." Pp. 55–79 in *High technology, space and society*, edited by M. Castells. Beverly Hills, CA: Sage Pub.

Gordon, R.L. 1980. *Interviewing: Strategies, techniques and tactics*. Dorsey Press.

Granovetter, Mark S. 1992. 'Economic Institutions as Social Constructions: A Framework for Analysis." *Acta Sociologica* 35:3-11

Grant, II, D.S. and R. Hutchinson. 1996. "Global smokestack chasing: A comparison of the state-level determinants of foreign and domestic manufacturing investment." *Social Problems,* 43(1):21–38.

Grant, II, D.S. and M. Wallace. 1994. "The Political economy of manufacturing growth and decline across the American states, 1970–1985." *Social Forces* 73:33–63.

Greensboro News & Record. December 20, 1997. "Pillowtex buys out Fieldcrest, joins nation's top linen makers."

Gullickson, G.L. 1986. *The Spinners and workers of Auffay: Rural industry and the sexual division of labor in a French village, 1750–1850*. NY: Cambridge University Press.

Gubrium, J.F. and J.A. Holstein. 1987. "The private image: Experiential location and method in family studies." *Journal of Marriage and the Family* 49:773–786.

Habermas, J. 1984. *The theory of communicative action. Volume one: Reason and the rationalization of society*, translated by Thomas McCarthy. Boston, MA: Beacon Press.

Hall, J.D. 1986. "Disorderly women: Gender and labor militancy in the Appalachian South." *Journal of American History* 73:354–82.

Hall, J.D., J. Leloudis, R. Korstad, M. Murphy, L.A. Jones, and C.B. Daly. 1987. *Like a family: The making of a southern cotton mill world.* Chapel Hill: University of North Carolina.

Hamel, J. 1993. *Case study methods.* Thousand Oaks, CA: Sage Pub.

Hamilton, D. (ed.). 1990. *The Uruguay Round, textiles trade and the developing countries.* Washington, DC: World Bank.

Harrison, B. and B. Bluestone. 1988. *The great U-turn: Corporate restructuring and the polarizing of America.* NY: Basic Books.

Hartmann, H. 1976. "Capitalism, patriarchy, and job segregation by sex." *Signs* 1:137–69.

——— 1981. "The unhappy marriage of Marxism and feminism: Towards a more progressive union." Pp. 1–41 in *Women and the revolution,* edited by L. Sargent. Boston, MA: South End Press.

Harvey, D. 1982. *The limits to capital.* Chicago, IL: University of Chicago Press.

——— 1985. *The urbanization of capital: Studies in the history and theory of capital urbanization.* Baltimore, MD: Johns Hopkins University Press.

——— 1989. *The condition of postmodernity: An enquiry into the origins of cultural change.* Cambridge, MA: Basil Blackwell.

Herring, H.L. 1929. *Welfare work in mill villages: The story of extra-mill activities in North Carolina.* Chapel Hill: University of North Carolina Press.

——— 1977/1949. *The passing of the mill village: A revolution in a southern institution.* Westport, CN: Greenwood Press.

Hill, R.C. 1987. "Global factory and company town: The changing division of labor in the international automobile industry." Pp. 18–37 in *Global restructuring and territorial development,* edited by J. Henderson and M. Castells. Newbury Park, CA: Sage Pub.

Hoover's Handbook Database. 1996. Austin, TX: The Reference Press, Inc.

Huberman, M. and M.B. Miles. 1994. "Data management and analysis method." Pp. 428–444 in *Handbook of qualitative research,* edited by N.K. Denzin and Y.S. Lincoln. Thousand Oaks: Sage Publications.

Jackman, M. 1994. *The velvet glove: Paternalism and conflict in gender, class, and race relations.* Berkeley, CA: University of California Press.

Jackson, B. 1987. *Fieldwork.* Urbana, IL: University of Illinois Press.

Jaffee, D. 1986. "The political economy of job loss in the United States, 1970–1980." *Social Problems* 33:297–315.

Janiewski, D. 1985. *Sisterhood denied: Race, gender, and class in a new South community.* Philadelphia, PA: Temple University Press.

Johnson, L.C. 1990. "New patriarchal economies in the Australian textile industry." *Antipode* 22(1):1–32.

Juravich, T. 1985. *Chaos on the shop floor: A workers view of quality, productivity, and management.* Philadelphia, PA: Temple University Press.

Kanter, R.M. 1995. *World class: Thriving locally in the global economy.* NY: Simon and Schuster.

Kearns, P.R. 1995. *Weavers of Dreams.* Barium Springs, NC: Mullen Press.

Kennett, P. 1994. "Exclusion, post-Fordism and the 'New Europe.'" Pp. 14–32 in *Economic restructuring and social exclusion,* edited by P. Brown and R. Crompton. London: UCL Press Limited.

Killian, M.S. and S.L. Porterfield. 1994. *The North American Free Trade Agreement: Identifying adversely affected industries and local labor markets.* Working draft.

Killian, M.S. and C.M. Tolbert. 1993. "Mapping social and economic space: the delineation of local labor markets in the US." Pp. 69–79 in *Inequalities in labor market areas* edited by J. Singelmann and F.A. Deseran. Boulder CO: Westview Press.

Lamphere, L. 1987. *From working daughters to working mothers: Immigrant women in a New England industrial community.* Ithaca, NY: Cornell University Press.

Lamphere, L. (ed.). 1992. *Structuring diversity: Ethnographic perspectives on the new immigration.* Chicago, IL: University of Chicago Press.

Lamphere, A.S. and G. Grenier (eds.). 1994. *Newcomers in the workplace: Immigrants and the restructuring of the U.S. economy.* Philadelphia: Temple University Press.

Leach, B. and A. Winson. 1995. "Bringing globalization down to earth: Restructuring labor in rural communities." *Canadian Review of Sociology and Anthropology* 32(3):341-364

Lee, C.K. 1995. "Engendering the worlds of labor: Women workers, labor markets, and production politics in the South China economic miracle." *American Sociological Review,* 60:378–397.

Leiter, J. 1982. "Continuity and change in the legitimation of authority in southern mill towns." *Social Problems* 29:540–50.

———— 1986. "Reaction to subordination: Attitudes of southern textile workers." *Social Forces* 64:948–74.

Leiter, J., M. Schulman, and R. Zingraff. 1991. *Hanging by a thread: Social change in southern textiles.* Ithaca, NY: ILR Press.

Lobao, L. 1993. "Renewed significance of space in social research: Implications for labor market studies." Pp. 11–32 in *Inequalities in Labor Market Areas,* edited by J. Singelmann and F.A. Deseran. Boulder, CO: Westview Press.

———— 1996. "A sociology of the periphery versus a peripheral sociology: Rural sociology and the dimension of space." *Rural Sociology* 61(1):77–102.

Lobao, L.M. and M.D. Schulman. 1991. "Farming pattern, rural restructuring, and poverty: a comparative regional analysis." *Rural Sociology* 56:562–602.

Lofland, J. 1971. *Analyzing social settings: A guide to qualitative observation and analysis.* Belmont, CA: Wadsworth Pub. Co.

Lyson, T.A., D. Harper, and G. Gillespie. 1994. "Economic embeddedness and rural livelihood strategies." Unpublished Manuscript, Ithaca, NY: Cornell University.

Mahon, R. 1984. *The politics of industrial restructuring: Canadian textiles.* Toronto: University of Toronto Press.

Marcus, G.E. "What comes (just) after 'post'? The case of ethnography." Pp. 563–574 in *Handbook of qualitative research*, edited by N.K. Denzin and Y.S. Lincoln. Thousand Oaks, CA: Sage Publications Pub.

Martinsville Bulletin. February 28, 1995.

Martinsville Bulletin. September 5, 1995.

Marx, K. 1857–1858/1964. *The Grundrisse: foundations of the critique of political economy.* NY: International Publishers.

────── 1976. *Capital.* Vol. 1. Harmondsworth, Eng.: Penguin Books.

────── 1977. *Capital.* Vol. 3. Moscow: Progress Books.

────── 1978. *Capital.* Vol. 2. Harmondsworth, Eng.: Penguin Books.

Massey, D. and R. Meegan. 1979. "The geography of industrial reorganisation." *Progress in Planning* 10:155–273.

────── (eds.). 1985. *Politics and methods: Contrasting studies in industrial geography.* London; New York: Methuen.

McConnell, J. and A. MacPherson. 1994. "The North American Free Trade area: An overview of issues and prospects." Pp. 163–187 in *Continental trading blocs: The growth of regionalism in the world economy,* edited by R. Gibb and W. Michalak. NY: J. Wiley.

McLaurin, M.A. 1971. *Paternalism and protest: Southern mill workers and organized labor, 1875–1905.* Westport, CT: Greenwood Pub. Corp.

McMichael, P. 1994. *Development and social change: A global perspective.* Thousand Oaks, CA: Pine Forge Press.

────── 1994b. "Introduction: Agro-food system restructuring: Unity in diversity." Pp. 1–18 in *Global restructuring of agro-food systems*, edited by P. McMichael. Ithaca: Cornell University Press.

────── 1994c. "Global restructuring: Some lines of inquiry." Pp. 277–300 in *Global restructuring of agro-food systems*, edited by P. McMichael. Ithaca: Cornell University.

────── 1996. "Globalization: Myths and realities." *Rural Sociology* 61(1):25–55.

McNamara, A. and P. Snelling. 1995. *Design and practice for printed textiles.* Melbourne: Oxford University Press.

Merton, R.K., M. Fiske, P.L. Kendall (eds.). 1990. *The focused interview: A manual of problems and procedures,* 2nd ed. NY: Free Press.

Miles, M. and M. Huberman. 1994. *Qualitative analysis for social scientists.* Cambridge: Cambridge University Press.

Miles, M. 1994. *Qualitative data analysis.* Thousand Oaks, CA: Sage Publications, Inc.

Mingione, E. 1991. *Fragmented societies: A sociology of economic life beyond the market paradigm.* Cambridge, MA: Basil Blackwell Ltd.

────── 1994. "Life strategies and social economies in the Postfordist age." *International Journal of Urban and Regional Research* 18(1):24–45.

Mitchell, B. 1921. *The rise of the cotton mills in the South.* Baltimore, MD: Johns Hopkins University Press.

Michael, G.S. 1931. *Textile unionism and the South.* Chapel Hill, NC: University of North Carolina.

Moore, J. and L. Wingate. 1940. *Cabarrus reborn: A historical sketch of the founding and development of Cannon Mills and Kannapolis.* Kannapolis, NC: Kannapolis Pub. Co.

Myers, K. 1996. *Sailing under false colors: Race, class, and gender in a women's organization.* Ph.D. Dissertation, North Carolina State University, Raleigh, NC.

New York Times. June 25, 1999. "Union victory at plant in South is labor Milestone."

Newby, H. 1975. "The deferential dialectic." *Comparative studies in society and history* 17:139–64.

——— 1977. *The deferential worker: A study of farm workers in East Anglia.* London: Penguin Books.

——— 1980. "Textile workers in a tobacco county: A comparison between yarn and weave mill villages." Pp. 345–368 in *The southern common people: Studies in nineteenth century social history,* edited by E. Magdol and J.L. Wakelyn. Westport, CN: Greenwood Press.

——— 1981. "The myth of the contented southern mill worker." Pp. 187–204 in *Perspectives on the American South: Annual review of society, politics, and culture, Volume 1,* edited by M. Black and J.S. Reed. NY: Gordon and Breach Science Press.

Newman, D. 1978. "Work and community life in a southern textile town." *Labor History* 19:204–25.

North Carolina Department of Commerce, State Data Center, MIS Section, EDIS Unit. 1997. *Cabarrus County Profile.* Web Site Address: http://cmedis.commerce.state.nc.us/cmedis /outlook/cabacp.pdf

Penn, R. 1990. *Class, power and technology: skilled workers in Britain and America.* Oxford: Polity Press.

——— 1991. "Technical change and gender relations in contemporary Rochdale." In *Gender and employment in modern Britain,* edited by A. Scott. Oxford: Oxford University Press.

Penn, R. and J. Leiter. 1991. "Employment patterns in the British and US textile industry: A comparative analysis of recent changes." Pp. 139–162 in *Hanging by a thread,* ed. by J. Leiter, M. Schulman, and R. Zingraff. Ithica, NY: ILR Press.

Piore, M.J. and C.F. Sabel. 1984. *The second industrial divide: Possibilities for prosperity.* NY: Basic Books.

Pope, L. 1942. *Millhands and preachers: A study of Gastonia.* New Haven, CT: Yale University Press.

Potwin, M.A. 1927. *Cotton mill people of the Piedmont: a study in social change.* NY: Columbia University Press.

Punch, M. 1994. "Politics and ethics in qualitative research." Pp. 83–97 in *Handbook of qualitative research,* edited by N. Denzin and Y. Lincoln. Thousand Oaks, CA: Sage Pub.

Raleigh News & Observer. August 14, 1997. "Cannon employees reject union."

Raleigh News & Observer. September 1, 1985. "Kannapolis: Still feeling change at Cannon."

Raleigh News & Observer. September 6, 1995. "Fieldcrest ordered to make changes."

Rankin, Edward L. 1987. *Cannon Mills Company 1887–1987: A century of progress.* Kannapolis, NC: Fieldcrest Cannon, Inc.

Raynolds, L.T. 1994. "Institutionalizing flexibility: A comparative analysis of Fordist and post-Fordist models of Third World agro-export production." Pp. 143–162 in *Commodity chains and global capitalism,* edited by G. Gereffi and M. Korzeniewicz. Westport, CT: Greenwood Press.

Roscigno, V.J. and C.D. Anderson. 1995. "Subordination and struggle: Social movement dynamics and processes of inequality." *Perspectives on Social Problems* 7:249–274.

Roscigno, V.J. and M.K. Kimble. "Elite power, race and the persistence of low unionization in the South." *Work & Occupations* 22(3):271–300.

Roscigno, V.J. and D. Tomaskovic-Devey. 1994. "Racial politics in the contemporary South: Toward a more critical understanding." *Social Problems* 41:585–607.

Rubinstein, R.L. 1987. "Stories told: In-depth interviewing and the structure of its insights." In *Qualitative gerontology,* edited by L. Leinharz and G. Rowlles. NY: Springer.

Salmond, J.A. 1995. *Gastonia 1929: The story of the labor mill strike.* Chapel Hill, NC: University of North Carolina Press.

Sassen, S. 1990. "Economic restructuring and the American city." *Annual Review of Sociology* 16:465–90.

———— 1994. *Cities in a world economy.* Thousand Oaks, CA: Pine Forge Press.

Schor, J.B. 1992. *The overworked American: The unexpected decline of leisure.* NY: Basic Books.

Schott, J.J. 1994. *The Uruguay Round: An assessment.* Washington, DC: Institute for International Economics.

Schulman, M.D. and C.D. Anderson. 1993. "Political economy and local labor markets: Toward a theoretical synthesis." Pp. 33–48 in *Inequalities in labor market areas,* edited by J. Singelmann and F.A. Deseran. Boulder, CO: Westview Press.

Schulman, M.D. and C.D. Anderson. 1999. "The dark side of the force: A case study of restructuring and social capital." *Rural Sociology* 64(3):351-372

Schulman, M.D. and J. Leiter. 1991. "Southern textiles: Contested puzzles and continuing paradoxes." Pp. 3–20 in *Hanging by a thread: Social change in southern textiles.* Edited by J. Leiter, M. Schulman, and R. Zingraff. Ithaca, NY: ILR Press.

Schulman, M.D., R. Zingraff, and L. Reif. 1985. "Race, gender, class consciousness and union support: An analysis of southern textile workers." *Sociological Quarterly* 26:187–204.

Scott, A.F. 1970. *The southern lady: From pedestal to politics, 1830–1930.* Chicago: University of Chicago Press.

Simon, B. 1991. "Choosing between the ham and the union: Paternalism in the Cone Mills of Greensboro, 1925–1930." Pp. 81–100 in Hanging *by a thread: Social change in southern textiles,* edited by J. Leiter, M. Schulman, and R. Zingraff. Ithaca, NY: ILR Press.

Singlemann, J. and F.A. Deseran (eds.). 1993. *Inequalities in labor market areas.* Boulder, CO: Westview Press.

Sklar, H. 1995. *Chaos or community? Seeking solutions, not scapegoats, for bad economics.* Boston, MA: South End Press.

Smith, D.E. 1986. "Institutional ethnography: a feminist method." *Resources for Feminist Research* 15(1):6–38.

Spradley, J.P. 1979. *The ethnographic interview.* NY: Holt, Rinehart and Winston.

Stake, R.E. 1994. "Case studies." Pp. 236–247 in *Handbook of qualitative research,* edited by N. Denzin and Y. Lincoln. Thousand Oaks, CA: Sage Publications.

Standard & Poor's. 1987. *Standard & Poor's industry surveys.* NY: Standard & Poor's.

———— 1988. *Standard & Poor's industry surveys.* NY: Standard & Poor's.

———— 1992. *Standard & Poor's industry surveys.* NY: Standard & Poor's.

Stanley, K. 1994. "Industrial and labor market transformation in the US meat packing industry." Pp. 129–145 in *Global restructuring of agro-food systems,* edited by P. McMichael. Ithaca, NY: Cornell University Press.

Stone, G. and J. Heffner. 1995. *The uprising of '34.* Video documentary produced at SUNY-Stony Brook.

Stuart, A.W. 1993. *Cabarrus County: An overview.* Draft prepared for the Cabarrus County Sharing the Vision Executive Committee. Charlotte, NC: UNC-Charlotte.

Taplin, I.M. 1994. "Strategic reorientations of US apparel firms." Pp. 205–223 in *Commodity chains: Global capitalism,* edited by G. Gereffi and M. Korzeniewicz. Westport, CT: Greenwood Press.

Taplin, I.M. and J. Winterton. 1996. "Contradictory forces for change in a labor intensive industry." Draft prepared for presentation at North Carolina State University Department of Sociology, Raleigh, NC.

Taylor J.S. and R. Bogdan. 1984. *Introduction to qualitative research methods: The search for meanings.* NY: Wiley & Son, Inc.

Thompson, H.M. 1906/1971. *From the cotton field to the cotton mill: A study of the industrial transition in North Carolina.* NY: Macmillan.

Tickamyer, A.R. 1996. "Sex, lies, and statistics: Can rural sociology survive restructuring? (or) What is right with rural sociology and how can we fix it?" *Rural Sociology* 61(1):5–24.

Tickamyer, A.R. and C.M. Duncan. 1990. "Poverty and opportunity structure in rural America." *Annual Review Sociology* 16:67–86.

Tolbert II, C.M., J .J. Beggs, and G. D. Boudreaux. 1995. *PUMS-L data and associated files: CD-Rom edition.* (Machine-readable data files)/prepared by the Louisiana Population Data Center, Louisiana State University and LSU Agricultural Center. Baton Rouge: The Center.

Tolbert II, C.M. and M.S. Killian. 1987. *Labor market areas for the US.* Washington, DC: US Department of Agriculture.

Tomaskovic-Devey, D. 1993. *Gender and racial inequality at work: The sources and consequences of job segregation.* Ithaca, NY: ILR Press.

Tomaskovic-Devey, D. A. Kalleberg, and P. Marsden. 1995. "Organizational patterns of gender segregation" In *Studying organizations,* edited by A. Kalleberg, P. Marsden, J. Spaeth, and D. Knoke. Thousand Oaks: Sage.

Tomaskovic-Devey, D. and V.J. Roscigno. 1996. "Racial economic subordination and white gain in the US South." *American Sociological Review* 61(4):565–589.

Toyne, B., J.S. Arpan, A.H. Barnett, D.A. Ricks, T.A. Shimp, J.E. Andrews, J.C. Clamp, C.D. Rogers, G. Shepherd, T.V. Tho, E.A. Vaughn, S. Woolcock. 1984. *The global textile industry.* Boston: Allen & Unwin.

Tuchman, G. 1994. "Historical social science: Methodologies, methods and meaning." Pp. 306–323 in *Handbook of qualitative research,* ed. by N. Denzin and Y. Lincoln. Thousand Oaks, CA: Sage.

Tullos, A. 1989. *Habits of industry: White culture and the transformation of the Carolina Piedmont.* Chapel Hill, NC: University of North Carolina Press.

U.S. Bureau of the Census. 1996. *Statistical Abstract of the United States.* Washington D.C.: U.S. Government Printing Office.

Vallas, S.P. 1993. *Power in the workplace: The politics of production at AT&T.* Albany, NY: SUNY Press.

—— 1993b. "Workers, firms, and the dominant ideology: Hegemony and consciousness in the monopoly core." *The Sociological Quarterly* 32(1):1–83.

Vallas, S. and J.P. Beck. 1996. "The transformation of work revisited: The limits of flexibility in American manufacturing." *Social Problems* 43(3):339–361.

Wall Street Journal. August 12, 1996.

Wall Street Journal. March 4, 1996.

Webb, E.J., D.T. Campbell, Richard D. Schwartz, and Lee Sechrest. 1966. *Unobtrusive measures: Nonreactive research in the social sciences.* Chicago, IL: Rand McNally.

Weber, M. 1903–1917/1949. *The methodology of the social sciences,* edited by E. Shils and H. Finch. NY: Free Press.

West, C. and S. Fenstermaker. 1995. "Doing difference." *Gender & Society* 9(1):8–37.

Williamson, J. 1984. *The crucible of race: Black/White relations in the American South since emancipation.* NY: Oxford University Press.

Wood, P.J. 1986. *Southern capitalism: The political economy of North Carolina, 1880–1980.* Durham, NC: Duke University Press.

—— 1991. "Determinants of industrialization on the North American 'periphery.'" Pp. 58–80 in *Hanging by a thread: Social change in southern textiles,* edited by J. Leiter, M.D. Schulman, and R. Zingraff. Ithaca, NY: ILR Press.

Yin, R.K. 1993. *Application of case study research.* Newbury Park, CA: Sage.

—— 1994. *Case study research: Design and methods,* 2nd ed., Thousand Oaks, CA: Sage.

Young, M.W. (ed.). 1963. *Textile leaders of the South*. Columbia, SC: The R.L. Bryan Company.

Zey, M. 1993. *Banking on fraud: Drexel, junk bonds, and buyouts*. NY: Aldine de Gruyter.

Zingraff, R. 1991. "Facing extinction?" Pp. 199–216 in *Hanging by a thread: Social change in southern textiles*, edited by J. Leiter, M. Schulman, and R. Zingraff. Ithaca, NY: ILR Press.

Zuboff, S. 1988. *In the age of the smart machine: The future of work and power*. NY: Basic Books.

Index